English

Escalate

7

M000117417

Copyright © by Houghton Mifflin Harcourt Publishing Company

All rights reserved. No part of this work may be reproduced or transmitted in any form or by any means, electronic or mechanical, including photocopying or recording, or by any information storage and retrieval system, without the prior written permission of the copyright owner unless such copying is expressly permitted by federal copyright law. Requests for permission to make copies of any part of the work should be addressed to Houghton Mifflin Harcourt Publishing Company, Attn: Intellectual Property Licensing, 9400 Southpark Center Loop, Orlando, Florida 32819-8647.

Printed in the U.S.A.

ISBN 978-0-544-57898-2

12 0877 21

4500826201   B C D E F G H

If you have received these materials as examination copies free of charge, Houghton Mifflin Harcourt Publishing Company retains title to the materials and they may not be resold. Resale of examination copies is strictly prohibited.

Possession of this publication in print format does not entitle users to convert this publication, or any portion of it, into electronic format.

Cover, Title Page Photo Credits: Escalator ©Rodrigo Apolaya/APU Imagenes/Getty Images. All Other Photos ©HMH

Escalate  English

Student Activity Book

7

Unit 1

BOLD ACTIONS

SELECTIONS

BUILD VOCABULARY

HOW ENGLISH WORKS

PERFORMANCE TASK

Unit 2

PERCEPTION AND REALITY

SELECTIONS

BUILD VOCABULARY

HOW ENGLISH WORKS

PERFORMANCE TASK

Unit 3

NATURE AT WORK

SELECTIONS

BUILD VOCABULARY

HOW ENGLISH WORKS

PERFORMANCE TASK

Unit 4

RISK AND EXPLORATION

SELECTIONS

BUILD VOCABULARY

HOW ENGLISH WORKS

PERFORMANCE TASK

Unit 5

THE STUFF OF CONSUMER CULTURE

SELECTIONS

BUILD VOCABULARY

HOW ENGLISH WORKS

PERFORMANCE TASK

Unit 6

GUIDED BY A CAUSE

SELECTIONS

BUILD VOCABULARY

HOW ENGLISH WORKS

PERFORMANCE TASK

Table of Contents

Bold Actions

A ship in harbor is safe, but that is not what ships are built for.

—John A. Shedd, writer

What do you think of when you imagine "bold actions"? Use images to create visual notes, or write down your ideas.

What jobs call for bold actions? Explain why workers who do these jobs must act boldly.

_____

_____

_____

The word *foolhardy* means "reckless or impulsive." Foolhardy actions are usually bold, too. What are some differences between brave, heroic acts and bold but foolhardy ones?

_____

_____

_____

How do you feel before you do something bold? How do you feel during your bold action? How do you feel afterwards?

_____

_____

_____

What kinds of bold actions can help you become a stronger, more confident person?

_____

_____

_____

Other notes about Bold Actions:

_____

_____

_____

© Houghton Mifflin Harcourt Publishing Company

Academic Vocabulary

As you work through Unit 1, look and listen for these words. Use them when you talk in class and in your writing. Write about your experiences using these words in the last column of the chart.

Word	Definition	Related Forms	My Experiences
aspect	a part of something		
cultural	• relating to the beliefs, customs, and art of a group of people • relating to the fine arts	culture, cultured, multicultural	
evaluate	to examine something carefully to judge its value or worth	evaluation, evaluator	
resource	something useful or helpful	resourceful, natural resources	
text	a book or other piece of writing	textbook, textual	

© Houghton Mifflin Harcourt Publishing Company

Many Words for Bold: Synonyms

Complete the word web. Use a print or online thesaurus to find more synonyms for *brave*, *daring*, *determined*, and *forceful*.

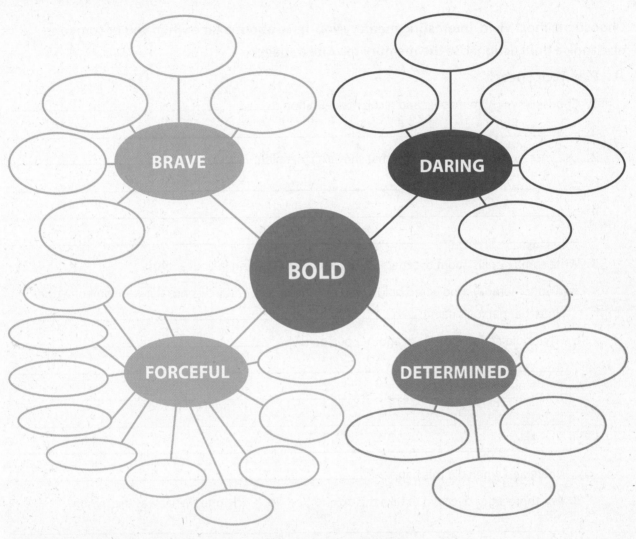

Finish each sentence with a synonym for *bold* from the word web.

1. Some dog trainers are willing to work with _____ dogs, but sometimes it is not possible to stop such dogs from attacking humans, other dogs, and other animals.

2. My sister was a very _____ toddler: she had run away from home twice by the time she was four years old.

3. Many fairy-tale heroes are _____ people who rescue others from dragons and other deadly imaginary creatures.

© Houghton Mifflin Harcourt Publishing Company

Speech About a Bold Action

To evaluate your speech, use the Presenting a Speech Rubric available from your online Student Resources or from your teacher.

Choose the most vivid, interesting memory you have about a time when you or someone else took a bold action. Use the memory to write a speech.

A. Plan Your Speech

1. Choose a synonym for *bold* and record its definition. _____
   _____

2. Use your synonym in a sentence that shows its meaning. _____
   _____
   _____
   _____

3. Write some details about the memory you will be describing in your speech.

   a. In your memory, who acted boldly, you or someone else? (Circle one.) If it was someone else, write that person's name: _____

   b. What bold action did you or another person take? _____
      _____
      _____
      _____
      _____

   c. Where and when did this happen? _____

   d. Was there a good reason to take this action? Yes. No. (Circle one.) What was the reason?
      _____
      _____

B. Write Your Speech Use the details above to write your speech on another sheet of paper. Keep your speech to about one page. Be sure to include:

- an attention-grabbing beginning
- an interesting middle that moves quickly along and includes only the important details
- an ending that sums up the memory you have described (For example, you might end by telling your listeners what you learned from the bold action you have described.)

© Houghton Mifflin Harcourt Publishing Company

Collaborative Discussion Support

Look through GoGirl's blog. Find information to complete the table. Make notes below.

What does GoGirl write about on April 16? (What happens <u>after</u> she hurts her knee and <u>before</u> she starts writing her blog?) _____

_____

_____

_____

What happens on April 17 and how does GoGirl feel? _____

_____

_____

_____

What happens on April 18 and 19 and how does GoGirl feel? _____

_____

_____

_____

_____

What happens on April 20 and 21 and how does GoGirl feel? _____

_____

_____

_____

What does GoGirl do on April 22? What happens on April 23 and how does GoGirl feel?

_____

_____

_____

_____

© Houghton Mifflin Harcourt Publishing Company

Build Vocabulary

Shades of Meaning

raced	sprinted	bolted	scurried	darted
trotted	jogged	scampered	dashed	

A. Complete the sentence by circling the synonym with the correct shade of meaning.

1. Katya _____ to the tree and back in under three minutes.

   a. trotted   **b.** raced

2. I was so excited that I _____ up the stairs when I heard the doorbell ring.

   a. dashed   **b.** jogged

3. He _____ over to the table to when he saw the glass starting to fall.

   a. scurried   **b.** bolted

4. The lizard _____ across the forest floor.

   a. sprinted   **b.** scampered

B. Using two words from the box, write two sentences that mean that someone is running slowly. Then, use two words from the box in two sentences about someone moving fast.

_____

_____

_____

_____

_____

_____

C. Choose four synonyms from the box. Write a sentence for each word that conveys the correct shade of meaning.

1. Word: _____

   Sentence: _____

2. Word: _____

   Sentence: _____

3. Word: _____

   Sentence: _____

4. Word: _____

   Sentence: _____

© Houghton Mifflin Harcourt Publishing Company

Start a Blog

To evaluate your blog, use the Blog Rubric available from your online Student Resources or from your teacher.

Pick Your Blog Topic Training to win a 10k race is so important to GoGirl that she writes a blog about it. Name three topics that are very important to you. These should be topics you would enjoy blogging about. After thinking it over, circle the topic you will blog about.

1. _____ 2. _____ 3. _____

Create Your Blog Title Now that you have picked your topic, invent a catchy, unique title for your blog. Your title should remind visitors of your topic, just as "GoGirl" reminds visitors that the blogger is a runner. (Hint: Most blog titles are short!)

_____

Give Yourself an Online Nickname It isn't safe for kids to reveal personal information (including real names) online, so make up a nickname for yourself. It is fine if your nickname is the same as your blog title, as GoGirl's is. _____

Think About Images for Your Blog Some blogs have photos, cartoons, and other kinds of images. What images do you want your blog to include?

_____

_____

_____

Think About Colors and Designs for Your Blog List some colors and designs for your blog.

_____

_____

Find a Host for Your Blog Ask your teacher for a list of free websites that host blogs. Visit some of these sites to see which one you like best. You can experiment with creating blogs before you choose a host. Which host did you pick? _____

Set Up Your Blog Use your ideas and information to set up your blog. Write your first entry. Next, email friends and family members. Send them a link to your new blog!

_____

_____

_____

_____

_____

_____

© Houghton Mifflin Harcourt Publishing Company

Idioms

A. **Read the underlined idioms from "GoGirl." Complete the sentence with the best answer.**

1. *Soon the other runners will be eating my dust!* indicates that the blogger is _____

   a. ahead of the others.　　　**b.** angry at the others.　　　**c.** laughing at the others.

2. *My legs are killing me* means the blogger's legs _____

   a. are her secret weapon.　　　**b.** are causing her pain.　　　**c.** are attacking her.

3. *All my muscles are screaming at me* conveys the idea that the blogger's muscles are _____

   a. looking at her.　　　**b.** picking on her.　　　**c.** hurting her.

4. *I took a different course than usual, one that had some mega hills to climb.*
   Mega hills are _____

   c. steep, high hills.　　　**a.** gently rolling hills.　　　**b.** craggy, rocky hills.

B. **Restate each sentence in your own words. Use context clues from the blog to help you understand what GoGirl means.**

1. Soon the other runners will be eating my dust!

   _____

   _____

2. It was a big bummer.

   _____

   _____

3. Pain city, population me!

   _____

   _____

C. **Choose two of the underlined idioms in A. Write a sentence for each idiom.**

1. Idiom: _____

   Sentence: _____

   _____

   _____

2. Idiom: _____

   Sentence: _____

   _____

   _____

© Houghton Mifflin Harcourt Publishing Company

Subject, Verb, Object

Complete the sections assigned to you by your teacher.

A. Read each sentence. Decide if the underlined word is a subject, verb, object, or none of the above.

1. <u>Tyrese</u> solved the equation.

   a. subject   **b.** verb   **c.** object   **d.** none of the above

2. The men and women ran <u>down</u> the stairs to the exit.

   a. subject   **b.** verb   **c.** object   **d.** none of the above

3. The security guard caught Isaac and <u>Dana</u> sneaking into the building.

   a. subject   **b.** verb   **c.** object   **d.** none of the above

4. Dr. Guzman <u>discussed</u> his research.

   a. subject   **b.** verb   **c.** object   **d.** none of the above

B. Complete each sentence with a word that fits.

1. Mr. Kowalski and his _____ caught lots of fish yesterday.

2. Ellen _____ a thoughtful argument about expectations.

3. Sunlight reflected off the _____ and the snow.

4. Remy and Matias pushed the _____ up the hill.

5. _____ gave a long speech.

C. Choose one topic and write a paragraph about it. Your paragraph should include: at least four sentences, at least one compound subject, and at least one compound object. Possible topics:

spotting an unusual animal around your neighborhood	learning to enjoy a new food	listening to new music

_____

_____

_____

_____

_____

_____

_____

© Houghton Mifflin Harcourt Publishing Company

Problem/Solution

Answer the questions about *Conner Stroud*.

1. What is Ana's assignment?

   _____

2. Who is Ana's subject?

   _____

3. What does Ana need to complete her assignment?

   _____

4. Why did Conner decide to be a tennis player?

   _____

5. What problem did Conner face to play tennis?

   _____

6. What solution did he find to this problem?

   _____

7. What is Conner's goal now?

   _____

8. What is Conner's message for kids who want to play sports but don't think they are good enough?

   _____

Compare and Contrast

Think about the video you have just seen. Compare and contrast it with "GoGirl."

1. How are GoGirl and Conner Stroud similar?

   _____

2. How are they different?

   _____

3. What common lesson do both the video and the blog want to teach?

   _____

© Houghton Mifflin Harcourt Publishing Company

Build Vocabulary

Critical Vocabulary

A. Read the sentences below. Circle the definition of each underlined word. Remember that you can look up any unfamiliar words in the dictionary.

1. We have to prepare a profile on someone whom we admire. *Profile* means

    a. collection.   **b.** series.   **c.** description.

2. I love tennis, so I looked for inspiration in the racket world. *Inspiration* means

    a. something that gives you an idea.

    b. something that is different.

    c. something that teaches you something.

3. Conner Stroud was born with no legs or hips. *Hips* means

    a. joints at the top of the legs.

    b. joints in the middle of the legs.

    c. joints at the bottom of the legs.

4. He dreamed of being a player and playing competitively. *Competitively* means

    a. trying to win against others.   **b.** badly.   **c.** testing your strength.

5. How do the other players react when they have to confront you on the court? *Confront* means

    a. avoid.   **b.** signal.   **c.** oppose.

B. Choose a word from the box to complete each sentence.

profile	inspiration	hips	prosthetic	competitively	courtside	confront

1. People with _____ legs can put them on and take them off.

2. The dancer's _____ have to be very flexible in order to kick so high.

3. I read a _____ of Nelson Mandela online.

4. At basketball games, people love to sit in the _____ seats.

5. Colleen plays video games _____.

6. My _____ for this report was my friend Ismael.

7. It's really tough when you _____ your brother on the other side of the net.

C. Choose three words from the box in Part B. Use each word in a sentence.

1. _____

2. _____

3. _____

© Houghton Mifflin Harcourt Publishing Company

Staying on Task

Make notes while you are reading "Smokejumpers: Parachuting Firefighters."

Were you able to stay focused as you read the article?

_____
_____
_____
_____

Did your attention wander? When?

_____
_____
_____
_____

What did you do to bring your mind back to the article?

_____
_____
_____
_____

What helpful tips about focusing on your reading can you share with classmates?

_____
_____
_____

Now that you have read the article, describe some of the skills that smokejumpers need to do their job.

_____
_____
_____
_____

© Houghton Mifflin Harcourt Publishing Company

Academic Vocabulary

A. Complete each sentence with the correct word(s) from the box.

| plot | its reliable public transportation | seeing her friends |

1. Ryan likes to say that the best aspect of living in New York is _____
_____.

2. Maria's favorite aspect of going to the park is _____.

3. One aspect of a novel is its _____.

B. Complete the answers with information from the text.

> Tom is finishing his report on a Mark Twain story. He is checking to see how many
> aspects of Twain's style he has covered. One aspect is the way the characters speak
> in a dialect. Another aspect is Twain's use of exaggeration to emphasize important
> ideas. The third aspect he wants to cover is the way the characters are introduced.

1. What is Tom checking his report for?

He's checking to see if he _____
_____.

2. What is the first aspect he wants to cover?

The first aspect is _____
_____.

3. What is another aspect?

Another aspect is _____
_____.

4. What is the third aspect?

The third aspect is _____
_____.

C. Using the word *aspect*, write a sentence about an aspect of life that would be different if
you were two years older than you are now.

_____
_____

Build Vocabulary

Critical Words

Choose four words from the word box below. Make a 4-square chart for each word you chose. Look up any unfamiliar words in the dictionary.

engulfed	inferno	intense	meadows	spotters	trainees

Definition	Part of Speech

WORD

Sentence	Synonyms

Definition	Part of Speech

WORD

Sentence	Synonyms

Definition	Part of Speech

WORD

Sentence	Synonyms

Definition	Part of Speech

WORD

Sentence	Synonyms

© Houghton Mifflin Harcourt Publishing Company

Collaborative Discussion Support

Look through the article. Find information to answer the questions below.

What skills do smokejumpers need? _____

_____

_____

_____

_____

_____

_____

_____

_____

_____

_____

Why are smokejumpers important? _____

_____

_____

_____

_____

_____

_____

_____

_____

_____

_____

_____

© Houghton Mifflin Harcourt Publishing Company

Analyze the Text

Use the hints to help you answer each question. Include evidence from the article that supports each of your answers.

Question 1	My Answer	Evidence from Lines 12–19
Draw Conclusions Reread the description of a smokejumper's physical requirements and activities in lines 12–19. What conclusions can you draw from this description?	_____ _____ _____ _____ _____ _____ _____ _____	_____ _____ _____ _____ _____ _____ _____ _____

Hints for Question 1: When you **draw conclusions** based on text, you use clues from the text along with information you already know to think of new ideas. As you answer Question 1, think about these points and questions:

- All firefighters are strong and skilled, even if they are not smokejumpers.
- Does being a smokejumper sound easier or harder than being a "regular" firefighter?
- If someone who is not already a regular firefighter wants to become a smokejumper, how likely is he or she to get the job?

Question 2	My Answer	Evidence from the Text
Author's Purpose What does the author want you to know about the importance of smokejumpers in the future?	_____ _____ _____ _____	_____ _____ _____ _____

Hint for Question 2: You can find the answer to this question in the last paragraph on page 12 of your **Student Book.**

© Houghton Mifflin Harcourt Publishing Company

Build Vocabulary

Compound Words

| hallway | doorknob | tabletop | signpost | gateway | paycheck | woodwork |

A. Look at the compound words. Write the two words that make up each compound word.

Compound Word	Word #1	Word #2
hallway		
doorknob		
tabletop		
signpost		
gateway		
paycheck		
woodwork		

B. Choose four compound words from the box above. Write sentences for each word. Underline the compound word.

1. _____
2. _____
3. _____
4. _____

C. Make three new compound words, each containing <u>one</u> word part from the compound words in the box below. Write a sentence for each word.

| woodwork | paycheck | hallway |

1. word: _____
   _____

2. word: _____
   _____

3. word: _____
   _____

© Houghton Mifflin Harcourt Publishing Company

Class Discussion

To Be or Not to Be a Smokejumper

Complete the chart to help you decide whether you would or wouldn't want to be a smokejumper. Think about the following aspects of smokejumping:

- high level of physical fitness
- skills you would need
- the danger of parachuting
- the danger of firefighting
- the growing need for smokejumpers

Good Things About Working as a Smokejumper	Bad Things About Working as a Smokejumper

© Houghton Mifflin Harcourt Publishing Company

Suffix -ee

Remember that some verbs can be made into nouns by adding the suffix -ee.

| awardee | employee | retiree | interviewee | appointee |

A. Find the verb contained in each noun and write it in the verb column of the table below.

Noun form	Verb
awardee	
employee	
interviewee	
retiree	
appointee	

B. Complete each sentence with a noun from the box.

1. Someone who's been awarded a prize is a(n) _____.

2. Someone who's employed at a company is a(n) _____.

3. Someone who's interviewed is a(n) _____.

4. Someone who's retired is a(n) _____.

5. Someone who's been appointed is a(n) _____.

C. Choose three words from the list. Use each word in a sentence. Underline the word.

1. _____
   _____
   _____

2. _____
   _____
   _____

3. _____
   _____
   _____

© Houghton Mifflin Harcourt Publishing Company

Object Pronouns

A. Decide which pronoun can replace the underlined word or phrase.
Circle the correct answer.

1. The boy protested against the group's policy.

   a. He   **b.** They   **c.** Him   **d.** We

2. Her dad taught Marcia how to program.

   a. she   **b.** him   **c.** them   **d.** her

3. Christine, Mabel, and I started a band.

   a. Us   **b.** We   **c.** They   **d.** She

4. Did you hear what happened to Eric and Rose?

   a. her   **b.** him   **c.** them   **d.** us

B. Fill in each blank with a pronoun that fits.

1. Could you buy _____ at the grocery store?

2. _____ pushed Matt into the lake.

3. _____ flew off the ramp.

4. I passed the ball to _____.

5. The ranger guided _____ around the camp.

C. Choose one topic and write four sentences about it. Include at least one plural subject pronoun, at least one plural object pronoun, at least one singular subject pronoun, and at least one singular object pronoun in your paragraph. You may choose your own topic.
Possible topics:

describe your favorite place to spend time with friends	describe a member of your family	how to deal with a cold

1. _____

   _____

2. _____

   _____

3. _____

   _____

4. _____

   _____

© Houghton Mifflin Harcourt Publishing Company

Academic Vocabulary

A. Complete each sentence with the correct word from the box.

cultural	cultured

1. Aisha gave a report about some of her country's _____ treasures.

multicultural	culture

2. Jean-Xavier says that France is almost as _____ as the United States.

culture	cultured

3. Melinda enjoys listening to the professor because he is so _____.

cultural	culture

4. Damien hopes his paintings make people want to learn more about the Mayan _____.

B. Read the passage and answer the questions.

> People of many different cultures lived in North America before the Europeans arrived. California was the most multicultural area, with more than 100 different Native American tribes. Each tribe had its own language and cultural traditions.

1. Who lived in North America before the Europeans arrived?

_____ lived in North America before the Europeans arrived.

2. What kind of area was California?

California was _____.

3. What did each tribe have?

Each tribe had _____.

C. Some aspects of culture are music, art, dance, theater, cooking, and literature. Use *culture* or *cultural* to write a sentence about the one you enjoy most.

_____

_____

© Houghton Mifflin Harcourt Publishing Company

Collaborative Discussion Support

Use the categories in the chart below to record the most important aspects of "Hercules: An Underground Rescue." Cite text examples to support your ideas. Include examples that show the real and supernatural aspects of the story.

Characters	Setting

Plot	Theme

© Houghton Mifflin Harcourt Publishing Company

Human Nature

Use the chart to organize your ideas for the Write On! assignment on p. 19 of the Student Book.

Hercules' bold and heroic actions express something about human nature. What lessons about human nature do we learn from his actions? Use examples from the story to complete the chart.

Hercules' Action	What We Learn About Human Nature
Hercules left his meal untouched and went to speak to the king.	
Hercules decides to go to the Underworld to find the queen.	
Hercules removes his indestructible cape and sword before he begins his journey to the Underworld.	
Hercules made an offering to Hermes before going to the Underworld.	
Hercules' voice trembles when he asks Hades to release the queen.	
Hercules wondered if he made a mistake.	
Hercules ordered the king and queen to prepare a banquet for Hades and reminded them they might not be so lucky next time.	

© Houghton Mifflin Harcourt Publishing Company

Build Vocabulary

Using Context Clues

A. Read the sentences below from the selection. Use context clues to answer each question. Circle the answer. Remember to use the dictionary to look up the definitions of unfamiliar words.

1. "I **acquiesce** to guide you as far as the entrance of the Underworld, but I despair of your chances." *Acquiesce* means

   a. to agree to   **b.** to be afraid of   **c.** to hesitate

2. "With a **decisive** nod of his head, Hercules proclaimed, 'Yes, I'm going to bring Alcestus back.'" *Decisive* means

   a. eager   **b.** determined   **c.** sarcastic

3. "'She must love you **immensely**,' Hercules said." *Immensely* means

   a. occasionally   **b.** a little bit   **c.** a great deal

4. "The *tink-tink-tink* was **emanating** from the tool in his hand." *Emanating* means

   a. shouting   **b.** returning   **c.** originating

5. "'Alcestus is an exceptionally just and good person. Her **voluntary** presence here proves that.'" *Voluntary* means

   a. cooperative   **b.** unwilling   **c.** timely

B. Write the word from the box that completes each sentence.

decisive	emanating	voluntary	immensely	acquiesce	descended

1. Will you _____ to my plan?

2. It was time to take _____ action.

3. It would help me _____ if you walked the dog today.

4. There's a weird smell _____ from the refrigerator.

5. Are you here on a _____ basis?

6. I watched as he slowly _____ into the cellar.

C. Rewrite each sentence from Part B using a word or phrase of your own. Make sure you keep the meaning of each sentence the same as the sentences in Part B.

1. Will you _____ to my plan?

2. It was time to take _____ action.

3. It would help me _____ if you walked the dog today.

4. There's a weird smell _____ from the refrigerator.

5. Are you here on a _____ basis?

6. I watched as he slowly _____ into the cellar.

© Houghton Mifflin Harcourt Publishing Company

Create a Cause-and-Effect Chart

While you listen to the Podcast, use the Cause-and-Effect organizer to take notes and to answer the following questions:

- What caused glassmakers to move to Murano?

- What effects resulted from glassmakers sharing their skills?

- Can you say what caused the invention of modern clear glass?
  Or do you think that there were many causes?

- Did the invention of clear glass cause anything else to happen?

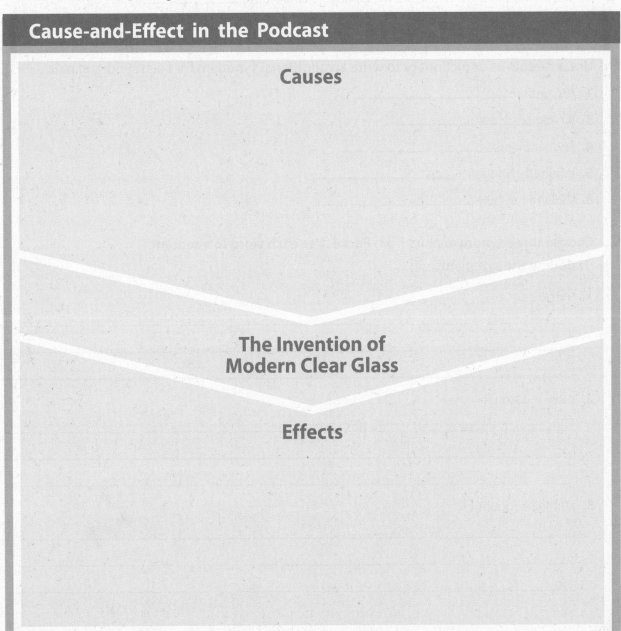

Cause-and-Effect in the Podcast

Causes

**The Invention of
Modern Clear Glass**

Effects

Synonyms

A. Replace each underlined word with a synonym from the box.

boundless	ill	joy	rescue	spare

1. She tried to <u>free</u> the rabbit from the trap. _____

2. Her smiling face showed her <u>happiness</u>. _____

3. The little girl's curiosity was <u>infinite</u>. _____

4. The star of the show is <u>sick</u> and will be unable to perform. _____

5. Please <u>save</u> my life, and I will grant you three wishes. _____

B. Use a thesaurus or dictionary to write an additional synonym for each synonym pair.

1. rescue/free _____

3. ill/sick _____

4. joy/happiness _____

5. infinite/boundless _____

6. sadly/mournfully _____

C. Choose three synonym pairs from Part B. Use each word in a sentence. Underline the synonyms.

1. sick/ill

_____

_____

_____

2. sadly/mournfully

_____

_____

_____

3. abundant/bountiful

_____

_____

_____

© Houghton Mifflin Harcourt Publishing Company

Listen and Analyze

Steven Johnson said that inventions can create "ripple effects" through history. The effects of one invention can cause a whole new set of changes and inventions. Use the graphic organizer to make notes about other inventions that created a "ripple effect."

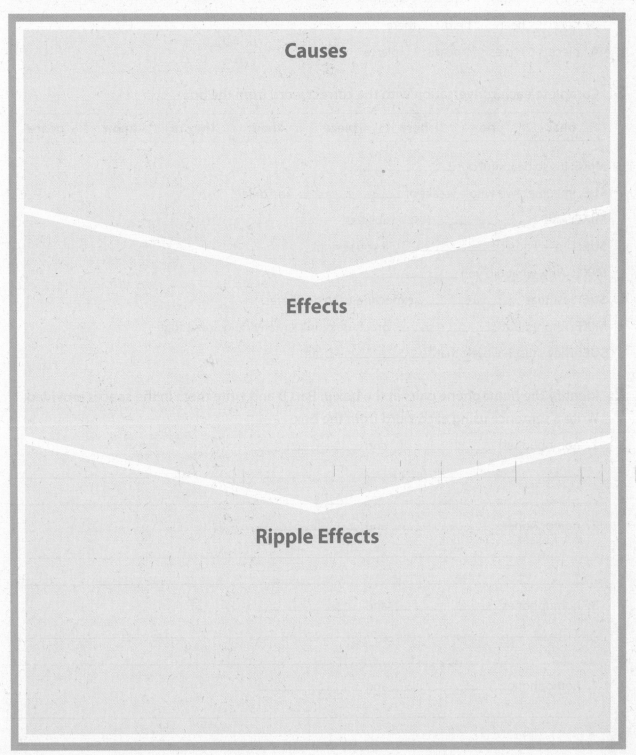

Causes

Effects

Ripple Effects

© Houghton Mifflin Harcourt Publishing Company

Homophones

A. Circle each homophone.

1. know   now   no   cow
2. they're   this   these   their
3. here   hear   herd   there
4. piece   pies   peace   pierce

B. Complete each conversation with the correct word from the box.

hear	no	here	piece	their	they're	know	peace

MIKE: It's so beautiful out _____!

SUE: Imagine! Two whole weeks of _____ and quiet!

MIKE: And _____ responsibilities!

SUE: Um— I don't _____ if you're right.

MIKE: Why, what did you _____?

SUE: Just that _____ expecting us to do chores.

MIKE: Chores! But _____ brochure didn't say anything about that!

SUE: They must have left that _____ out.

C. Identify the homophone pairs in the box in Part B and write them in the spaces provided. Write a sentence using each word from the box.

1. homophones: _____ and _____

_____

_____

2. homophones: _____ and _____

_____

_____

3. homophones: _____ and _____

_____

_____

4. homophones: _____ and _____

_____

_____

© Houghton Mifflin Harcourt Publishing Company

Verbs in the Future Tense

A. **What is the tense of the main verb in each sentence?**
Circle the correct answer.

1. The diagram shows how obesity rates have increased over time.

   a. present tense   **b.** present progressive tense   **c.** future tense   **d.** past tense

2. I think Louisa is right.

   a. future tense   **b.** present tense   **c.** past tense   **d.** past progressive tense

3. Michael talked about his day.

   a. present tense   **b.** future perfect tense   **c.** past tense   **d.** past progressive tense

4. Gordon will try to break the record tomorrow.

   a. future tense   **b.** future progressive tense   **c.** past tense   **d.** past perfect tense

B. **Complete each sentence with a verb, or verb phrase that makes sense in the context of the sentence.**

1. Grandmother _____ about what life was like when she was young. (past)

2. Rafael and I _____ you about the concert when we get back. (future)

3. That graph doesn't _____ what he says it does. (present)

4. Ariel and Clarence _____ each other with math and English. (present)

5. I _____ a tree to get a better view. (past)

C. **Choose one topic and write four sentences about it. Use at least one present tense verb, at least one future tense verb, and at least one past tense verb. You may choose your own topic. Possible topics:**

admitting a mistake	going ice skating	describe the story of your favorite book or movie

1. _____

2. _____

3. _____

4. _____

© Houghton Mifflin Harcourt Publishing Company

Critical Vocabulary

A. Read the sentences below. Circle the definition of each underlined word. Remember that you can look up any unfamiliar words in the dictionary.

1. His name <u>conjures up</u> images of warriors on horseback and unstoppable armies. *Conjures up* means

   a. ignores.   **b.** brings to mind.   **c.** makes clear.

2. His name conjures up <u>images</u> of warriors on horseback and unstoppable armies. *Images* means

   a. mental pictures.   **b.** people exercising.   **c.** military actions.

3. The empire of the Huns brought death and <u>destruction</u> to any who opposed them. *Destruction* means

   a. a big ship.   **b.** a slow-moving army.   **c.** a lot of damage.

4. The Roman Empire was a large and <u>formidable</u> empire. *Formidable* means

   a. very powerful.   **b.** very young.   **c.** abandoned.

5. The Huns forcibly pushed some <u>tribes</u> toward the Roman Empire. *Tribes* means

   a. political parties.   **b.** basketball teams.   **c.** groups of people.

6. The Huns were <u>nomads</u>, with no settled homes. *Nomads* means

   a. people who live in igloos.   **b.** people who sleep on camels.   **c.** people who move around.

B. Choose a word from the box to complete each sentence.

conjures up	images	destruction	nomads	formidable	tribes	tribute

1. There used to be many _____, but with all the borders and fences it's difficult for them to move around today.

2. The president traveled to the coast to see the _____ caused by the hurricane.

3. When I hear the word *Cinderella*, it _____ a vision of a glass slipper.

4. Some rulers demand crops or animals as _____ from people they conquer.

5. When European settlers arrived in America, they found many _____ of Native Americans.

6. When you read a book, you create your own _____ of the characters.

7. Huw is a _____ player on the tennis court.

C. Choose three words from the box in Part B. Use each word in a sentence.

1. _____
2. _____
3. _____

© Houghton Mifflin Harcourt Publishing Company

Academic Vocabulary

A. Complete each sentence with the correct word from the box.

evaluate	evaluating	evaluation

1. Marco is _____ several microwave ovens before deciding which one to buy.

evaluator	evaluated	evaluation

2. The mayor hired an _____ to study the way the city handles recycling.

evaluate	evaluating	evaluation

3. Mrs. Murrieta asked us to _____ the fire-drill procedure.

evaluation	evaluates	evaluator

4. Rin practiced every day at the pool to prepare for his swimming _____.

B. Read the passage and answer the questions using complete sentences.

> Alissa worked for a newspaper as a restaurant evaluator. She would visit different restaurants and write evaluations about them. She evaluated restaurants on their food, decorations, customer service, and cleanliness. Alissa's articles were very popular because she tried to be fair as well as funny.

1. What was Alissa's job?

_____

2. What types of things did she evaluate at a restaurant?

_____

_____

3. Why were Alissa's evaluations popular?

_____

C. How would you evaluate a new movie? Use a form of *evaluate* in your sentence.

_____

_____

_____

_____

© Houghton Mifflin Harcourt Publishing Company

Write an Opinion

Reread "Unstoppable Warriors." Then, complete the chart below to help you write your opinion.

Who do you think was bolder, Attila the Hun or Pope Leo?

I think _____ is bolder.
_____
_____
_____

Details in the Text That Support My Opinion
_____
_____
_____
_____
_____
_____
_____
_____
_____
_____
_____
_____

© Houghton Mifflin Harcourt Publishing Company

Critical Vocabulary

A. Read the sentences below. Circle the definition of each underlined word. Remember that you can look up any unfamiliar words in the dictionary.

1. The empire of the Huns brought death and destruction to any opponent who tried to fight them. *Empire* means

   a. group of nations controlled by one ruler.   **b.** mighty sword.   **c.** army on horseback.

2. The empire of the Huns brought death and destruction to any opponent who tried to fight them. *Opponent* means

   a. international organization.   **b.** political candidate.   **c.** one who fights against you.

3. By the late 300s CE, Rome's grip on many Mediterranean lands had weakened. *Grip* means

   a. control.   **b.** severe cold.   **c.** widespread hunting.

4. Due in part to pestilence and famine, Attila and the Hun army did not immediately move on to take Rome, but they stood poised to do just that. *Famine* means

   a. lack of money.   **b.** lack of food.   **c.** lack of horses.

5. Due in part to pestilence and famine, Attila and the Hun army did not immediately move on to take Rome, but they stood poised to do just that. *Poised* means

   a. pushed.   **b.** powerful.   **c.** ready.

6. Despite the terror of the Huns, the Pope went unarmed to speak with Attila. *Unarmed* means

   a. without problems.   **b.** without weapons.   **c.** without money.

B. Choose a word from the box to complete each sentence.

empire	opponent	centaurs	grip	famine	poised	unarmed

1. The bear lost its _____ on the branch and fell to the ground.

2. In Greek mythology, _____ were half-man half-horse creatures.

3. Maggie's _____ hit the ball hard right down the middle of the court.

4. When it doesn't rain in an area, crops won't grow, which may lead to a _____ .

5. The doctor decided to travel _____ because she thought people would understand that she wanted to help them.

6. An _____ grows by taking over nearby countries.

7. James stood on the platform, _____ to dive.

C. Choose three words from the box in Part B. Use each word in a sentence.

1. _____

2. _____

3. _____

© Houghton Mifflin Harcourt Publishing Company

Main and Subordinate Clauses

Complete each chart.

"Known for fantastically fast and strong horses, Hun warriors were such extraordinary riders that some people compared them to centaurs, mythical creatures that were half-man and half-horse." What is the main clause in this sentence from "Unstoppable Warriors"? What is the Subordinate Clause(s)?

Write a sentence below that has a main clause and a subordinate clause. Identify the clauses in the chart.

Main Clause	Subordinate Clauses

"Even Constantinople, the greatest city of the Eastern Roman Empire, made a payment, known as a tribute, to the Hun army rather than face hopeless destruction." What is the main clause in this sentence from "Unstoppable Warriors"? What is the Subordinate Clause(s)?

Write a sentence below that has a main clause and a subordinate clause. Identify the clauses in the chart.

Main Clause	Subordinate Clauses

© Houghton Mifflin Harcourt Publishing Company

Build Vocabulary

Prefix *un-* and Suffix *-less*

A. Circle the correct meaning of each word and write it in the space provided.

1. When something is *uneven* it is _____. straight jagged

2. An *unusual* object is one that is _____. rare ordinary

3. Someone who is *limitless* has _____. no limits a small limit

4. Something that is *worthless* is _____. expensive without value

B. Complete the sentences with the correct word from the box.
Look at the hints in parentheses.

aimless	breathless	cloudless	dreamless	restless
unafraid	uninhabited	unreal	untroubled	

It was a (no clouds) _____ night. I was feeling (fidgety) _____, so

I went out to the garden. It all felt (eerie) _____ somehow, as if I were on some

(deserted) _____ planet. I was calm and (not afraid) _____, however.

I wandered around in an (drifting) _____ state until I saw the sunrise. Only then did I

run (excited) _____ back to the house and into my bed, where I fell immediately into

an (pleasant) _____, (without dreams) _____ sleep.

C. Choose three words from the box in Part B. Write a sentence for each word. Then write a
sentence for the base word of each word you chose. Underline the words.

1. word: _____

   sentence: _____

   base word: _____

   sentence: _____

2. word: _____

   sentence: _____

   base word: _____

   sentence: _____

3. word: _____

   sentence: _____

   base word: _____

   sentence: _____

© Houghton Mifflin Harcourt Publishing Company

Critical Vocabulary

A. Read the sentences below. Circle the definition of each underlined word. Remember that you can look up any unfamiliar words in the dictionary.

1. Never let anyone lower your goals. *Goals* means

    a. number of points you score.   **b.** things you want to do.   **c.** grades in school.

2. Others' expectations of you are determined by their limitations of life. *Expectations* means

    a. beliefs about what you'll do.   **b.** rules for you to follow.   **c.** feelings towards you.

3. Others' expectations of you are determined by their limitations of life. *Determined* means

    a. cancelled.   **b.** feared.   **c.** influenced.

4. Others' expectations of you are determined by their limitations of life. *Limitations* means

    a. restrictions.   **b.** luck.   **c.** tragedies.

5. The sky is your limit, sons. *Limit* means

    a. what you spend.   **b.** maximum.   **c.** neighborhood.

B. Choose a word from the box to complete each sentence.

goals	expectations	determined	limitations	limit	hoop

1. The sailboat's direction and speed were _____ by the wind.

2. The speed _____ for cars near a school is 25 miles per hour.

3. If you set clear _____, you are more likely to achieve them.

4. We can't have more desks in the classroom because of space _____.

5. The coach's _____ for her team were very high.

6. Jason passed the ball to Phil, who was moving toward the _____.

C. Choose three words from the box in Part B. Use each word in a sentence.

1. _____

    _____

2. _____

    _____

3. _____

    _____

© Houghton Mifflin Harcourt Publishing Company

Progressive Verb Tense Clue Words

A. Identify the tense of the main verb in each sentence. Circle the correct answer.

1. Kimo will be leading the team while the captain is sick.

    a. future progressive tense   **b.** future tense
    c. present progressive tense   **d.** present tense

2. The ants were marching across the lawn.

    a. present tense   **b.** past perfect tense   **c.** past tense   **d.** past progressive tense

3. Are you talking to CJ?

    a. present progressive tense   **b.** present tense
    c. past progressive tense   **d.** future progressive tense

4. The explanation is confusing James.

    a. past progressive tense   **b.** future tense
    c. future progressive tense   **d.** present progressive tense

B. Fill in the blanks with a progressive tense verb that fits the context of the sentence. Use context clues to help you figure out what tense to use.

1. Mr. Chalabi _____ for election next fall.

2. I _____ to catch up on sleep last night.

3. Anna _____ trouble concentrating right now.

4. We _____ along the river when we saw the deer.

5. You _____ your work habits these days.

C. Choose one topic and write four sentences about it. In your paragraph, use at least one present progressive tense verb, at least one future progressive tense verb, and at least one past progressive tense verb. You may choose your own topic. Possible topics:

helping a friend	checking someone else's work for mistakes	getting something exciting in the mail

1. _____

2. _____

3. _____

4. _____

© Houghton Mifflin Harcourt Publishing Company

Academic Vocabulary

| resource | resources | resourceful | natural resources |

A. Choose the word from the box that best completes each sentence.

1. Diego knew that a government website would be a valuable _____ for his research.

2. Environmentalists work to protect our _____ .

3. We don't have the _____ to put on a science fair now, but we should start preparing for next year.

4. _____ people are never bored because they always find something interesting to do.

B. Read the passage and answer the questions.

> One of this country's great natural resources is our national parks and forests. If you decide to go far into the wilderness on a long hike, a map is an important resource. However, the trail is not always clear, so you'll have to be resourceful to get over or around the trees and rocks that can block your path.

1. What is one of this country's great natural resources?

   One of our great natural resources is _____.

2. What is an important resource when you go into the wilderness?

   _____ is an important resource.

3. Why will you have to be resourceful on the trail?

   You will have to be resourceful

   to _____.

C. Write a sentence about the resource you use most often when you do research. Use one of the words from the box.

_____

_____

_____

_____

_____

_____

© Houghton Mifflin Harcourt Publishing Company

Performance Task

Write a Narrative Poem

Use this page to organize your poem. Read the Performance Task directions on page 33 of the Student Book.

Theme
_____
_____
_____
_____

Storytelling Elements (characters, setting, plot)
_____
_____
_____
_____

Conflict
_____
_____
_____
_____

Point of View
_____
_____
_____
_____

Form
_____
_____
_____
_____

© Houghton Mifflin Harcourt Publishing Company

Figurative Language

A. Each sentence contains a figure of speech in boldface text. Complete each sentence with the answer that best defines the figure of speech. Circle the answer.

1. His career is **on the line** means his career is _____.
   a. in jeopardy   **b.** over   **c.** on the rise

2. When she said, "**The sky's the limit**!" she was talking about being _____.
   a. chatty   **b.** famous   **c.** stingy

3. My dad always told me to "**shoot for the sun**." I think that's why I'm so _____.
   a. motivated to succeed   **b.** scared of heights   **c.** easy to be with

4. Which of these would be "**like looking for a needle in a haystack**"?
   a. finding one sheet of paper in a huge pile of papers
   b. looking for an unfamiliar address   **c.** looking for a cow in a pasture

B. Complete the sentences with an idiom from the box.

on the line	shoot for the sun	like looking for a needle in a haystack	Fortune favors the brave	go ballistic

1. "Now go out there and play," said the coach. "Remember that the state championship is _____
   _____."

2. "_____!" called my mom to make me feel like I could do anything.

3. "In this house," said my Grandpa, "looking for my glasses is _____
   _____."

4. "Now don't _____," I warned my barking Chihuahua. "That dog is much bigger than you are!"

5. When I had to dive off the high board, my swimming instructor Told me not to be scared. He said,
   "Remember the saying: '_____.'"

C. Choose three figurative expressions from Part B. Write a sentence for each. Underline the expressions.

1. Figurative expression: _____
   Sentence: _____

2. Figurative expression: _____
   Sentence: _____

3. Figurative expression: _____
   Sentence: _____

© Houghton Mifflin Harcourt Publishing Company

Build Vocabulary

Critical Vocabulary

A. Read the sentences below. Circle the definition of each underlined word. Remember that you can look up any unfamiliar words in the dictionary.

1. Half compass, half clock, this device will keep track of the years traveled. *Compass* means

   a. tool for finding direction.   **b.** tool to predict weather.   **c.** satellite.

2. I'll tell you everything about my adventure, but please, no interruptions. *Interruptions* means

   a. exciting events.   **b.** breaking in while someone is speaking.   **c.** leaving until someone is finished.

3. The Eloi served immense perfumed fruits, which were completely new to me. *Immense* means

   a. tasty.   **b.** very red.   **c.** huge.

4. While still rejoicing over the reflection of the moon on the water, I faced the biggest mystery. *Reflection* means

   a. shininess.   **b.** image on a shiny surface.   **c.** disappearing light.

5. Would I encounter the ghost-like creatures I had once seen running on the hill? *Encounter* means

   a. meet.   **b.** scare.   **c.** attack.

6. I used another match to light a torch and start a fire to distract the Morlocks, who were after me. *Distract* means

   a. scare them away.   **b.** communicate with.   **c.** take their attention away from something.

B. Choose a word from the box to complete each sentence.

| compass | interruptions | immense | inhabiting | reflection | encounter | distract |

1. In ancient times, there were many different tribes _____ this area.

2. What would you do if you _____ a space alien?

3. Ms. Clinton said that she wanted to finish reading the story without any _____.

4. In a sandy desert, there are no landmarks so you need a _____ to figure out which way to go.

5. The cat was confused when it saw its _____ in the mirror.

6. Jeremy played chess with Diosdado to _____ him while his sister prepared his birthday surprise.

7. Mario put up an _____ tent where he would display his invention.

C. Choose three words from the box in Part B. Use each word in a sentence.

1. _____
2. _____
3. _____

© Houghton Mifflin Harcourt Publishing Company

Visual Clues

A. For each item, circle the best answer. You can use the art and the text in "The Time Machine" to help you.

1. The Time Traveler saw that the Eloi were <u>unintelligent</u>. *Unintelligent* means _____.

   a. super smart   **b.** friendly   **c.** foolish

2. The Time Traveler showed his <u>prototype</u> to the group of scientists. A *prototype* is _____.

   a. a model   **b.** a Sphinx   **c.** a well

3. The Time Traveler believed the Eloi had <u>devolved</u> as a species. *Devolved* means _____.

   a. collapsed   **b.** gone backwards   **c.** achieved success

4. The Time Traveler moved the <u>lever</u> and the Time Machine took off. A *lever* is _____.

   a. a brake   **b.** a device   **c.** an invention

5. The Time Traveler lit a torch to <u>distract</u> the Morlocks. *Distract* means _____.

   a. trick   **b.** frighten   **c.** sidetrack

B. Use the underlined words in A to complete the following sentences.

1. The Wright brothers developed an early _____ of an airplane.

2. The _____ jammed, making takeoff nearly impossible.

3. He might look _____, but he's really brilliant.

4. Don't _____ me when I'm trying to do my homework!

5. The scientists watched in horror as the mouse _____ into a prehistoric being.

C. Write a sentence for three of the underlined words from A.

1. Word: _____

   Sentence: _____

   _____

2. Word: _____

   Sentence: _____

   _____

3. Word: _____

   Sentence: _____

   _____

© Houghton Mifflin Harcourt Publishing Company

Verbs in the Future Perfect Tense

A. Identify the tense of the main verb in each sentence. Circle the correct answer.

1. I have made a presentation before.

   a. present tense   **b.** future tense   **c.** present perfect tense   **d.** past perfect tense

2. I had read my email before I got there, so I knew what to expect.

   a. future perfect tense   **b.** present perfect tense   **c.** past tense   **d.** past perfect tense

3. Arnaud has been back to Haiti twice so far.

   a. past perfect tense   **b.** future perfect tense

   c. past progressive tense   **d.** present perfect tense

4. Ms. Zimmerman will have finished writing her book by December.

   a. future perfect tense   **b.** present perfect tense

   c. future progressive tense   **d.** future tense

B. Fill in the blanks with a verb that fits the context of the sentence. Use context clues and the tense in parentheses to help you figure out what tense to use.

1. The executives _____ in protest when they failed to fix the problem. (past perfect)

2. Sam and I _____ to our state senator by Friday. (future perfect)

3. Mikki _____ about this topic many times. (present perfect)

4. Rosalind _____ home when there was a knock on the door. (past perfect)

5. Jerome _____ several mountains. (present perfect)

C. Choose one topic and write four sentences about it. Use at least one present perfect tense verb, at least one future perfect tense verb, and at least one past perfect tense verb. You may choose your own topic. Possible topics:

figuring out how to make a device work	going to a museum	riding a train

1. _____

2. _____

3. _____

4. _____

© Houghton Mifflin Harcourt Publishing Company

Suffix -ly

A. Read the sentences below from "The Time Machine." For each underlined word, write the base word underneath.

1. Looking for the missing Time Machine, the Time Traveler became <u>suddenly</u> tired.

   Base word: _____

2. The fruits eaten by the Time Traveler were <u>completely</u> new to him.

   Base word: _____

3. The Time Traveler had many questions, <u>particularly</u> about the wells.

   Base word: _____

4. <u>Clearly</u>, the future was not a paradise.

   Base word: _____

5. The Time Traveler <u>vaguely</u> remembered seeing some shadows.

   Base word: _____

6. The Time Traveler <u>quickly</u> learned that they called themselves the Eloi.

   Base word: _____

B. Use the underlined words in A to complete the following sentences.

1. If we walk _____ I think we'll make the show in time.

2. It was not a _____ cold day, but I was chilled to the bone.

3. I _____ froze, convinced I was being watched.

4. I _____ remembered I was supposed to be somewhere.

5. I _____ did not mean to imply that.

6. I am _____ thrilled to see you after all this time!

C. Choose a word with the suffix -ly from Part B. Write a sentence using the word. Then, identify the base word and use it in a sentence.

1. Word: _____

   Sentence: _____

   _____

   Base Word: _____

   Sentence: _____

   _____

© Houghton Mifflin Harcourt Publishing Company

Short Story Ideas

A. Circle the items in each box that you find interesting or exciting. Write at least three sentences about why you find these activities interesting and/or exciting.

Realistic	Fantasy
piloting a plane	exploring outer space
exploring somewhere new	digging for buried treasure
inventing a new product	slaying a dragon
learning something new	fighting a villain

Example:

I think _____ is interesting.

I think _____ is exciting.

_____

_____

_____

_____

_____

B. Write three ideas about situations for your short story. Remember, you can use a real experience, a fictional one, or a combination.

Idea 1 _____

_____

Idea 2 _____

_____

Idea 3 _____

_____

© Houghton Mifflin Harcourt Publishing Company

Plan Your Story

To evaluate your story, use the Short Story Rubric available from your online Student Resources or from your teacher.

Conflict

What is the problem or struggle that your characters face? _____

_____

Characters

The main character is _____

Other characters are _____

Describe what your main character looks like. _____

_____

Describe your main character's personality. _____

_____

Setting

Describe the place. _____

_____

Describe the time (daytime, nighttime, season, past, present, future) _____

_____

Point of View

First person: I, We

Third person: He, She, They

Which point of view will you use? _____

_____

_____

_____

_____

_____

© Houghton Mifflin Harcourt Publishing Company

Academic Vocabulary

| text | textual | textbook |

A. Complete each sentence with a word from the box.

1. Can you show me any _____ evidence to support your opinion?

2. A _____ usually contains many chapters, a glossary, and an index for students.

3. This _____ is interesting because the writer speaks in the second person.

B. Complete the sentences with your own choice of words.

1. Textual evidence is _____.

2. An instruction manual is considered _____ text.

3. If you write your opinion about something, you are writing _____ text.

C. Choose two texts that you like and write a paragraph about each one. Describe what you like, and what kind of text it is. (Is it a descriptive text, an explanatory text, a narrative text, or a persuasive text?)

1. _____
_____
_____
_____
_____
_____

2. _____
_____
_____
_____
_____
_____

© Houghton Mifflin Harcourt Publishing Company

Finalize Your Plan

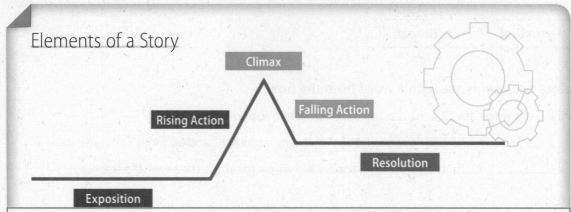

Elements of a Story

Exposition – Introduce your main character, setting, and conflict.

Rising Action – Introduce the obstacles the character must overcome. Build suspense.

Climax – The most important or exciting moment.

Falling Action – How the conflict is resolved and the lesson the character learns.

Resolution – The final part of the plot.

A. Review the elements of a story above. Describe the elements that you will include in your short story.

Exposition _____

_____

Rising Action _____

_____

Climax _____

_____

Falling Action _____

_____

Resolution _____

_____

B. Write a brief summary of your story.

_____

_____

_____

© Houghton Mifflin Harcourt Publishing Company

Build Vocabulary

Vocabulary Review

Here are some of the words you learned in this unit. Choose words from this list and sort them into the categories below. There are many possible correct answers!

aimless	destruction	hallway	scampered
appointee	determined	inferno	scurried
awardee	devolve	infinite	signpost
boundless	doorknob	inhabiting	tabletop
brave	dreamless	interruption	trainee
breathless	emanating	interviewee	unafraid
clearly	empire	multicultural	unarmed
compass	employee	nomads	uninhabited
completely	engulfed	opponent	untroubled
confident	expectations	particularly	vaguely
courageous	famine	plucky	voluntary
courtside	fearless	poised	woodwork
culture	forceful	profile	
daring	gatekeeper	prosthetic	
descend	gutsy	prototype	

Words with Prefixes

1. _____
2. _____
3. _____
4. _____
5. _____

Compound Words

1. _____
2. _____
3. _____
4. _____
5. _____

Words that Signify People

1. _____
2. _____
3. _____
4. _____
5. _____

Synonyms for "Brave"

1. _____
2. _____
3. _____
4. _____
5. _____

© Houghton Mifflin Harcourt Publishing Company

Easily Confused Words

A. **Circle the correct word in each sentence. Use the context clues to help you decide.**

1. I (advise, advice) you not to put sealed bottles in the freezer.

2. The committee is trying to (device, devise) a way to get Congress to listen to us.

3. Some people understand problems better when they explain their thought process (aloud, allowed).

4. Professor Lenski watched bacteria (adapt, adopt) to new conditions.

B. **Fill in the blanks with the correct word that fits the context of each sentence.**

1. Mark _____ his friend's attitudes.

2. Some nurses are _____ to prescribe certain medicines.

3. Some mathematicians _____ answers to complicated problems by imagining moving parts.

4. If not for batteries, many of the _____ we rely on would never have worked.

5. When Larry asked people online for help, he got a lot of bad _____.

C. **Write four sentences, one using *advice* or *advise*, one using *device* or *devise*, one using *aloud* or *allowed*, and one using *adapt* or *adopt*. Your sentences should demonstrate your understanding of the meaning of each word.**

1. _____
   _____
   _____

2. _____
   _____
   _____

3. _____
   _____
   _____

4. _____
   _____
   _____

© Houghton Mifflin Harcourt Publishing Company

Perception and Reality

I am not at all the sort of person you and I took me for.

— Jane Carlyle, writer

What does the word *perception* mean to you? Use images to create visual notes or write down your ideas.

What influences our perceptions?

_____

_____

What might change our perceptions?

_____

Why might our perceptions be wrong?

_____

Do we always know when our perceptions are wrong? Explain your answer.

_____

Other notes about perceptions:

_____

_____

_____

_____

_____

_____

© Houghton Mifflin Harcourt Publishing Company

Academic Vocabulary

As you work through Unit 2, look and listen for these words. Use them when you talk in class and in your writing. Write about your experiences using these words in the last column of the chart.

Word	Definition	Related Forms	My Experiences
abnormal	different or unexpected; not normal	normal	
feature	• an important part of something • to present or promote	featured, feature article	
focus	• to concentrate • to make an image clear	focused	
perceive	• to notice or become aware • to think of someone or something in a particular way	perception, misperception, perceptive	
task	a job or assignment	multitask	

© Houghton Mifflin Harcourt Publishing Company

Not the Same in Every Way: Homographs

Add another pair of homographs to the chart. Here are some words you might use: *close, does, lead, tear, wind*. If you are unsure of the meanings, check a dictionary. Complete all three sections of the chart. Be sure to write two complete sentences that show the meanings of both words in the Example column.

Word, Pronunciation, and Part of Speech	Meaning	Example
read (1) /rēd/ *(v.)*	to examine and grasp the meaning of (written or printed characters, words, or sentences)	I take out books from the library once a week so I always have something to **read**.
read (2) /rĕd/ *(v.)*	to have examined and grasped the meaning of (written or printed characters, words, or sentences)	I told my friend that I **read** the best book last night.
live (1) /lĭv/ *(v.)*	to be alive, exist; to reside, dwell	I **live** with my mom and my brother in our little house.
live (2) /līv/ *(adj.)*	involving performers or spectators who are physically present	I attended a **live** concert and the music boomed so loudly!
minute (1) /mĭn'ĭt/ *(n.)*	a unit of time equal to one-sixtieth of an hour, or 60 seconds	Class will be over in one **minute**.
minute (2) /mī-noot'/ *(adj.)*	exceptionally small, tiny	There is a **minute** chance the teacher will postpone the quiz today.

Finish each sentence with a homograph from the chart. To show which word in the pair is correct, put the number beside the word, such as read 1.

1. The greenhouse was filled with _____ butterflies.

2. Will you _____ that story to your little brother?

3. I just need a _____ of your time.

4. Where did you _____ before you moved here?

5. I see a _____ amount of sugar on your fingers.

6. I think I already _____ that book.

© Houghton Mifflin Harcourt Publishing Company

Perception Speech

To evaluate your speech, use the Presenting a Speech Rubric available from your online Student Resources or from your teacher.

Choose a topic for a short speech. Think about something that seems to change depending on how it is perceived. For instance, you could choose the optical illusions discussed in Browse magazine, or other situations you may know about.

Plan

1. Choose your topic. The illusion or situation I chose is _____.

2. Tell about it! Why is this topic interesting to you? Why will it interest your readers?

    _____

3. What sources will you check for information on your topic?

    _____

    _____

Prepare

Use your plan to prepare your speech. A well-organized speech is easier to remember.

1. Start by grabbing your listeners' attention. What will make them want to hear what you have to say?

    _____

2. What are your main points? What do you want your listeners to understand and remember?

    _____

3. Put your points in an order that will make them easy for listeners to understand.

    _____

4. How will you end your speech? Will you summarize your main points? Will you ask a question for your

    listeners to think about? _____

Tips for Giving a Speech

- Take several deep breaths and relax. Remember, your audience wants you to do well.
- Speak clearly. Don't go too fast or too slow.
- Make eye contact with your listeners.
- Smile!

USE WITH STUDENT BOOK p. 51 AND BROWSE MAGAZINE.

© Houghton Mifflin Harcourt Publishing Company

Collaborative Discussion Support

Look through "School Daze." Find information to answer the questions below.

What was the blogger's opinion about magic shows in the beginning of the post?

_____
_____
_____
_____
_____

What happened during the show that helped convince the blogger that his or her opinion was correct?

_____
_____
_____
_____
_____

What changed the blogger's mind about magic shows?

_____
_____
_____
_____
_____

What might this blogger write about next?

_____
_____
_____
_____
_____

© Houghton Mifflin Harcourt Publishing Company

Build Vocabulary

Critical Vocabulary

A. Read the sentences below. Circle the definition of each underlined word. Remember that you can look up any unfamiliar words in the dictionary.

1. Today, in <u>assembly</u>, it was Magic Show day. *Assembly* means

   a. the principal's office.　**b.** school meeting.　**c.** government building.

2. Anything is better than last week's video about <u>pedestrian</u> safety. *Pedestrian* means

   a. dog walking.　**b.** person watching television.　**c.** person walking.

3. She came down from the stage and started high-fiving kids up and down the <u>aisles</u>. *Aisles* means

   a. passages for walking between sections.　**b.** lamp posts.　**c.** walls at the back.

4. "This is your card!" she <u>announced</u>. *Announced* means

   a. said publicly.　**b.** signed.　**c.** understood.

5. I started to feel a little <u>panicked</u>. *Panicked* means

   a. welcome.　**b.** more disappointed.　**c.** worried and confused.

B. Choose a word from the box to complete each sentence.

assembly	pedestrian	aisles	deck	shuffled	auditorium

1. Hutchinson said that a musical group would play at today's _____ .

2. John walked up and down the _____ of the store looking for the cereal.

3. When you're a _____ , you should cross the street at the corner.

4. Since it was still raining and we couldn't go out, Debbie _____ the cards for another game.

5. My dad packed a _____ of cards so we could play Go Fish on our train trip.

6. The choir has to practice in the _____ before the concert.

C. Choose three words from the box in Part B. Use each word in a sentence.

1. _____

   _____

2. _____

   _____

3. _____

   _____

© Houghton Mifflin Harcourt Publishing Company

Blog

To evaluate your blog, use the Blog Rubric available from your online Student Resources or from your teacher.

Plan

1. Choose your topic. The suggestions on **Student Book** pages 54 and 55 might give you some ideas.

   The topic I chose is _____ .

   _____

   _____

2. Tell about it!

   Why is this topic interesting to you? Why will it interest your readers?

   _____

   _____

   _____

3. What sources will you check for information on your topic?

   _____

   _____

   _____

4. What kinds of files or links might you include in your blog?

   _____

   _____

   _____

Prepare

Use the information on your plan to prepare your blog.

1. Think of a catchy name for your blog that will grab readers' attention. What will you name it?

   _____

2. What main points will you include in your first blog? Don't try to cover them all! Focus on one or two main points, along with supporting details.

   _____

3. How will you end your blog? Will you encourage others to comment on it?

   _____

© Houghton Mifflin Harcourt Publishing Company

Multiple-Meaning Words

A. Choose the word(s) that correctly defines each underlined word.

1. We stood on the <u>deck</u> and watched the dolphins play.

   a. a full set of playing cards   **b.** platform on a ship

2. It was a <u>trick</u> meant to convince Ellen to give him all her money .

   a. a mischievous act   **b.** a practice meant to deceive or defraud

3. Louise is a valuable employee, and it will be <u>hard</u> to replace her.

   a. difficult   **b.** solid or firm

4. Ned has a very broad <u>chest</u>.

   a. the front part of the body between the neck and the stomach   **b.** a container for holding things

5. Ten <u>volunteers</u> offered to work at the soup kitchen.

   a. people who offer to do something   **b.** offer to do something

B. Define each underlined word.

1. Arlene took the book off the shelf but forgot to put it <u>back</u>. _____

2. Marla landed with a thud on the <u>hard</u> concrete. _____

3. I know a good <u>trick</u> for getting rid of grass stains. _____

4. The pirates hid the treasure <u>chest</u> on a deserted island. _____

5. Karen loves to play <u>tricks</u> on people. _____

| hard | trick | back | deck | chest |

C. Choose two words from the box. Use each word in two sentences that show different meanings of the word.

1. Sentence 1: _____

   _____

   Sentence 2: _____

   _____

2. Sentence 1: _____

   _____

   Sentence 2: _____

   _____

© Houghton Mifflin Harcourt Publishing Company

How English Works

Subject Complements

A. Decide if the underlined adjective is an article, a descriptive adjective, a quantitative adjective, or a subject complement. Circle the correct answer.

1. <u>The</u> tree fell down loudly.

   a. article   **b.** descriptive adjective   **c.** quantitative adjective   **d.** subject complement

2. The <u>tall</u> man touched the ceiling.

   a. article   **b.** descriptive adjective   **c.** quantitative adjective   **d.** subject complement

3. Tom unfocused his eyes until he saw <u>four</u> dots instead of two.

   a. article   **b.** descriptive adjective   **c.** quantitative adjective   **d.** subject complement

4. The little dog appears <u>excited</u>.

   a. article   **b.** descriptive adjective   **c.** quantitative adjective   **d.** subject complement

B. Fill in the blanks with an adjective that fits. Look at the specific part of speech in parentheses to pick the correct word.

1. The baby sounds _____. (subject complement)

2. The _____ person in line had vanished. (quantitative adjective)

3. Climbing the _____ hill left me winded. (descriptive adjective)

4. _____ animal scurried across the road. (article)

5. _____ animals can recognize themselves in a mirror. (quantitative adjective)

C. Choose one topic and write four sentences about it. Include at least one article, at least one descriptive adjective, at least one quantitative adjective, and at least one subject complement in your sentences. Possible topics:

adopting a new pet	**going on a road trip**
getting glasses for the first time	**describe your neighborhood**

1. _____

   _____

2. _____

   _____

3. _____

   _____

4. _____

   _____

© Houghton Mifflin Harcourt Publishing Company

Finding Information

Answer the questions about *Is It Magic?*

1. Why are the students coming into the room? _____

2. What is the purpose of their assignment? _____

3. What is the definition of perception they use in the video?

   _____

4. What is the definition of reality they use in the video?

   _____

5. Why do they think a magician is a good representation of perception and reality?

   _____

6. What is Adrian's perception of magic?

   _____

7. What is "the oldest trick in the book"? _____

8. What are some of the tricks the Great Doobini performs with the cups and balls?

   _____

   _____

   _____

   _____

9. How does magic relate to perception and reality?

   _____

10. How does Adrian's perception of magic change?

    _____

    _____

Compare and Contrast

Think about the video you have just seen. Compare and contrast it with "Abracadabra."

1. What common theme do the video and the blog share?

   _____

2. How are the characters Adrian, in the video, and the writer of School Daze similar? _____

   _____

© Houghton Mifflin Harcourt Publishing Company

Critical Vocabulary

A. Read the sentences below. Circle the definition of each underlined word. Remember that you can look up any unfamiliar words in the dictionary.

1. The Great Doobini is an amazing <u>magician</u>. *Magician* means

   a. person who does magic.   **b.** person who cares for children.   **c.** person who plans parties.

2. When we talk about reality, we mean the true <u>situation</u> that exists. *Situation* means

   a. all of the people who play on a team.   **b.** everything you have to learn in one year.

   c. what is happening at a particular time and place.

3. You don't believe the magician can trick you? I guess we'll just have to <u>convince</u> you. *Convince* means

   a. teach you how it's done.   **b.** get you to believe it.   **c.** bring you back to reality.

4. I hear we have a <u>skeptic</u> among us. *Skeptic* means

   a. expert.   **b.** king.   **c.** doubter.

B. Choose a word from the box to complete each sentence.

magician	situation	convince	skeptic	offense	effective

1. Don't be angry. Melvin didn't mean any _____.

2. Sydney doesn't think this plan will work, and she's not the only _____.

3. This _____ is famous for disappearing right before your eyes.

4. Sam is learning how to be a more _____ pitcher in softball.

5. An actor's job is to _____ you that he's really the character in the film.

6. We found ourselves in a very difficult _____ after it snowed for ten hours.

C. Choose three words from the box in Part B. Use each word in a sentence.

1. _____

   _____

2. _____

   _____

3. _____

   _____

© Houghton Mifflin Harcourt Publishing Company

Academic Vocabulary

A. Decide if each description is normal or abnormal and complete the chart. Write *normal* or *abnormal* after each description.

Description	Normal/Abnormal
blue mashed potatoes	
a giraffe with wings	
sweating after playing basketball	
feeling thirsty after running	
feeling sleepy after eating a big meal	

B. Complete the answers with words from the text.

> The patient looked normal as he sat in the doctor's waiting room—that is, until a fly began buzzing around. Then he started sweating and turned an abnormal shade of blue. He jumped up on the chair and covered his face. The receptionist came out with a flyswatter and quickly killed the fly. The man's color quickly became normal as he sat down again. The other patients went back to reading their magazines.

1. How did the patient look as he sat in the waiting room?

   The patient _____.

2. When the fly began buzzing, what became abnormal about him?

   He started _____.

3. After the receptionist swatted the fly, what happened to the man?

   His color _____.

C. Write one sentence using *normal* and one sentence using *abnormal*.

1. _____

   _____

2. _____

   _____

© Houghton Mifflin Harcourt Publishing Company

Critical Vocabulary

A. Read the sentences below. Circle the definition of each underlined word. Remember that you can look up any unfamiliar words in the dictionary.

1. Most carnivorous plants <u>evolved</u> to grow in damp places like swamps or bogs. *Evolved* means

   a. changed little by little.   **b.** suddenly lost control.   **c.** moved around a lot.

2. Plants take <u>nutrients</u> from the soil through their roots. *Nutrients* means

   a. beans for cooking.   **b.** sand and dirt.   **c.** things needed to stay alive.

3. Many carnivorous plants release tempting smells, or resemble other flowers, to <u>lure</u> their prey in. *Lure* means

   a. attract.   **b.** adapt.   **c.** buzz.

4. As scientists learn more all the time, our <u>notions</u> of what plants can do will be ever-changing. *Notions* means

   a. opportunities.   **b.** ideas.   **c.** criticisms.

B. Choose a word from the box to complete each sentence.

digest	evolved	nutrients	prey	lure	notions

1. Eagles and hawks hunt their _____ from high in the air.

2. Dogs have _____ into many shapes and sizes.

3. People's _____ about the solar system have changed greatly over the centuries.

4. Human beings can't _____ grass very well.

5. Beans provide many _____ that humans need.

6. Window displays are designed to _____ shoppers into the store.

C. Choose three words from the box in Part B. Use each word in a sentence.

1. _____

   _____

2. _____

   _____

3. _____

   _____

© Houghton Mifflin Harcourt Publishing Company

Collaborative Discussion Support

Organize your thoughts to compare and contrast two types of carnivorous plants mentioned in the article. What do they eat? How do they get their food? Cite text evidence to support your ideas.

How are two plants in the selection the same?	Cite text evidence.
_____	_____
_____	_____
_____	_____
_____	_____
_____	_____

How are two plants in the selection the different?	Cite text evidence.
_____	_____
_____	_____
_____	_____
_____	_____
_____	_____

Now answer these questions:

How did the information in this selection change how you perceive plants?	_____ _____
What else would you like to learn about carnivorous plants?	_____ _____
Would you like to have one of these plants at home? Why or why not?	_____ _____

USE WITH STUDENT BOOK pp. 58–61

© Houghton Mifflin Harcourt Publishing Company

Build Vocabulary

Vocabulary Strategy: Reference Aids

A. Answer the questions about each dictionary entry.

> **litigate** (lĭt′ ĭ-gāt′) *verb* 1. to subject to legal proceedings 2. to engage in legal proceedings
> **litigable   litigation   litigator**

1. What part of speech is *litigate*? _____

2. How many definitions does the dictionary give for *litigate*? _____

3. What related words does the entry show? _____

> **scowl** (skoul) *verb* 1. to wrinkle or contract the brow as an expression of anger or strong disapproval subject to legal proceedings
> *noun* 1. a look of anger or strong disapproval
> **scowler   scowlingly**

4. What part(s) of speech is scowl? _____

5. How many definitions does the dictionary give for scowl? _____

6. What related words does the entry show? _____

B. Choose two words from the selection "The Giver" and look them up in a print or digital dictionary. Provide information about each entry.

1. Word _____

Part of Speech _____

Definition _____

_____

2. Word _____

Part of Speech _____

Definition _____

_____

C. Use each word you looked up in Part B in a sentence.

1. _____

2. _____

© Houghton Mifflin Harcourt Publishing Company

Critical Vocabulary

A. Read the sentences below. Circle the definition of each underlined word. Remember that you can look up any unfamiliar words in the dictionary.

1. When you saw the faces take on color, it wasn't as deep or <u>vibrant</u> as the apple. *Vibrant* means

   a. tasty.   **b.** very green.   **c.** very bright.

2. Jonas listened, trying hard to <u>comprehend</u>. *Comprehend* means

   a. sing along.   **b.** believe.   **c.** understand.

3. I wish language were more <u>precise</u>. *Precise* means

   a. exact.   **b.** lucky.   **c.** broad.

4. You have the <u>capacity</u> to see beyond. *Capacity* means

   a. disease.   **b.** ability.   **c.** glasses.

5. You'll <u>gain</u> wisdom, then, along with colors. *Gain* means

   a. get more.   **b.** understand.   **c.** face.

B. Choose a word from the box to complete each sentence.

tones	vibrant	genetic	comprehend	precise	capacity	gain

1. On the game show, people have to guess the _____ price of a car.

2. When people taste this new watermelon, it will quickly _____ popularity.

3. The snow seems to take on red _____ when the sun sets.

4. Scientists can do a _____ study of you using your fingernail.

5. Scientists now have the _____ to create new species.

6. Ched didn't _____ the seriousness of his mistake.

7. The rocks in the canyon are a _____ orange.

C. Choose three words from the box in Part B. Use each word in a sentence.

1. _____

   _____

2. _____

   _____

3. _____

   _____

© Houghton Mifflin Harcourt Publishing Company

Absolute Adjectives

A. Decide if each sentence contains an example of an adjective phrase, compound adjective, comparative/superlative adjective, or absolute adjective. Circle the correct answer.

1. The desk had a rough, unfinished surface.
   - **a.** adjective phrase
   - **b.** compound adjective
   - **c.** comparative/superlative adjective
   - **d.** absolute adjective

2. We reached a unanimous decision to help out.
   - **a.** adjective phrase
   - **b.** compound adjective
   - **c.** comparative/superlative adjective
   - **d.** absolute adjective

3. Glass is hard but fragile.
   - **a.** adjective phrase
   - **b.** compound adjective
   - **c.** comparative/superlative adjective
   - **d.** absolute adjective

4. The ocean is wetter than fog.
   - **a.** adjective phrase
   - **b.** compound adjective
   - **c.** comparative/superlative adjective
   - **d.** absolute adjective

B. Complete each sentence with an adjective that fits. Use the adjective form in parentheses.

1. That spotlight is _____. (comparative adjective)

2. The deep ocean is _____. (compound adjective)

3. A _____ apple sat on the desk. (adjective phrase)

4. This version of my paper is pretty good, but I want to do more research before writing the _____ version. (absolute adjective)

5. We found a _____ star. (adjective phrase)

C. Choose one topic and write four sentences about it. Include at least one adjective phrase, at least one compound adjective, at least one comparative or superlative adjective, and at least one absolute adjective in your paragraph. You may choose your own topic. Possible topics:

| your favorite movie | a visit to the doctor | a typical day at school |

_____

_____

_____

_____

© Houghton Mifflin Harcourt Publishing Company

Collaborative Discussion Support

Look through *The Giver*. Respond to each question below. Use your answers to prepare the collaborative discussion. (See page 67 of the Student Book.)

How does Jonas feel when he learns that the leaders of this society have kept color a secret? What does he tell The Giver?

_____

_____

_____

_____

_____

_____

Would Jonas have agreed to living in ignorance, and not even knowing about color? How do you know?

_____

_____

_____

_____

_____

_____

_____

Does Jonas think the well-being of his community is worth living in Sameness?

_____

_____

_____

_____

_____

_____

_____

© Houghton Mifflin Harcourt Publishing Company

Comparison-Contrast Chart

Listen to the "Lessons from the Perry Como Sundae Bar" podcast for the second time. Then work with a partner to complete two columns of this chart. Use your own experiences and perceptions to describe the characters. Other partners will probably describe them in different ways, based on their own experiences and perceptions.

Situation	Perceptions of Robert, grandson	Perceptions of Grandmother Rose and other residents
the Perry Como Sundae Bar in the common room of the nursing home		
being old		
dancing		

© Houghton Mifflin Harcourt Publishing Company

Academic Vocabulary

feature	features	featured

A. Choose the word from the box that best completes each sentence.

1. The art festival will _____ paintings and photos by 50 different artists.

2. Diagrams, charts, and pictures are visual text _____.

3. The newspaper website has cool _____ like 3-D maps, videos, and podcasts.

4. The runners from Kenya were _____ performers at the track meet.

B. Read the passage and answer the questions.

Danny is writing a report about Africa. He hopes it will be the feature article in the school newspaper. Africa has many spectacular features, such as Victoria Falls, the largest waterfall in the world, but Danny's report features Uganda with its many national parks and lakes. He is working on the computer, so he can include text features like photos and maps.

1. What does Danny hope his report will be?

   He hopes his report will be _____.

2. What is one spectacular feature of Africa?

   _____ is a spectacular feature of Africa.

3. Which country does the report feature?

   The report _____.

4. What kind of text features is Danny including?

   Danny is including _____.

C. Write a paragraph that describes the kind of performance you would feature if you were organizing a cultural event.

_____

_____

_____

_____

_____

_____

© Houghton Mifflin Harcourt Publishing Company

Podcast: "Lessons from the Perry Como Sundae Bar"

Changing Perceptions

Listen to "Lessons from the Perry Como Sundae Bar" for the third time. Then work with a partner to complete the charts below.

Part A

How did Robert's perceptions change?

	How Robert felt in the beginning of the podcast	How he felt by the end of the podcast
About the "old folks' home"		
About Grandma Rose		
About the Perry Como music		
About dancing		

Part B

Think of a time that you and someone else saw and heard the same thing at the same time. You had a completely different idea of what happened from the other person. Write about it in the chart below.

How did you feel?	How did someone else feel?	Why do you think your perceptions were different?

© Houghton Mifflin Harcourt Publishing Company

Critical Vocabulary

A. Read the sentences below. Circle the definition of each underlined word. Remember that you can look up any unfamiliar words in the dictionary. (These words are from the podcast "Lessons from the Perry Como Sundae Bar.")

1. A man jumped up, grasping at the end of the rope ladder. *Grasping* means

   a. holding.   **b.** leaping.   **c.** failing.

2. From the airplane he could see the deep chasm in the earth. *Chasm* means

   a. silence.   **b.** mountain.   **c.** hole.

3. She twirled a lock of hair around her little finger. *Twirled* means

   a. dropped.   **b.** spun.   **c.** held.

4. She presumed that Marianna was still at work when she saw that her car was not in the driveway. *Presumed* means

   a. forgot.   **b.** supposed.   **c.** felt glad.

5. The gym holds a special swimming class for its geriatric members. *Geriatric* means

   a. athletic.   **b.** fun.   **c.** senior.

B. Choose a word from the box to complete each sentence.

chasm	twirled	snowballed	grasped	presumed

1. The pothole seemed like a giant _____ to the truck driver.

2. Julio _____ that the office would open early in the morning.

3. The leaf _____ on the choppy surface of the water.

4. I _____ at the rope to keep the boat from floating away.

5. The minor problem _____ into a major disaster.

C. Choose three words from the box in Part B. Use each word in a sentence.

1. _____

   _____

2. _____

   _____

3. _____

   _____

© Houghton Mifflin Harcourt Publishing Company

Critical Vocabulary

A. Read the sentences below. Circle the definition of each underlined word. Remember that you can look up any unfamiliar words in the dictionary.

1. Women were almost never called *pharaoh*, but there was one underline exception. *Exception* means

   a. someone who is different from others.   **b.** Egyptian leader.   **c.** royal monkey who sat on the throne.

2. She even went as far as altering her appearance, wearing the ceremonial golden false beard of a pharaoh. *Altering* means

   a. ruining.   **b.** changing.   **c.** fixing.

3. She proclaimed herself to be the daughter of the god Amun-Re. *Proclaimed* means

   a. announced.   **b.** changed.   **c.** hid.

4. She asserted that her birth was miraculous. *Asserted* means

   a. commanded.   **b.** denied.   **c.** stated.

5. Throughout her rule, Hatshepsut oversaw a prosperous, victorious Egypt. *Prosperous* means

   a. unhappy.   **b.** rich.   **c.** free.

6. These paintings and inscriptions tell stories of her life. *Inscriptions* means

   a. words sung in a song.   **b.** words cut into stone.   **c.** prayers.

B. Choose a word from the box to complete each sentence.

divine	exception	altering	proclaimed
asserted	prosperous	inscriptions	

1. All the people, with one _____, stood up when the mayor walked in.

2. Raphael marched into city hall and _____ himself mayor.

3. The village was finally peaceful and _____, so many people wanted to live there.

4. In one ancient Egyptian city, people believed that cats were _____.

5. The volcano erupted, _____ the life of everyone who lived near it.

6. The governor _____ that the state would recover quickly.

7. Historians study the _____ on ancient Egyptian pyramids.

C. Choose three words from the box in Part B. Use each word in a sentence.

1. _____

2. _____

3. _____

© Houghton Mifflin Harcourt Publishing Company

Build Vocabulary

The Suffixes *-ance*, *-ous*, and *-ful*

victorious	prosperous	miraculous	appearance	powerful

A. Choose a word from the box to answer each question.

1. Which word means "successful, especially financially"? _____

2. Which word means "extraordinary, incredible"? _____

3. Which word means "the way someone looks"? _____

4. Which word means "winning"? _____

5. Which word means "having great influence and control"? _____

B. Complete each sentence with a word from the box.

1. Judging by his casual _____, Mark didn't know that he was attending a formal party.

2. The people treated members of the _____ army like heroes.

3. The _____ woman contributed money for many good causes.

4. Maria's sudden recovery was _____.

5. The _____ king ruled with an iron hand.

C. Choose three words from the box. Use each word in a sentence.

1. Word: _____

_____

_____

_____

2. Word: _____

_____

_____

_____

3. Word: _____

_____

_____

_____

© Houghton Mifflin Harcourt Publishing Company

Prepositional Phrases

Complete the sections assigned to you by your teacher.

A. Multiple Choice. Decide whether the underlined prepositional phrase is modifying the subject, the direct object, the subject complement, or the object of another prepositional phrase.

1. Mrs. Dyson put the book on the counter <u>near</u> the toaster.

   a. subject   **b.** direct object   **c.** subject complement   **d.** object of another prepositional phrase

2. Misha heard a noise <u>across</u> the hall.

   a. subject   **b.** direct object   **c.** subject complement   **d.** object of another prepositional phrase

3. My dad is the man <u>beside</u> the helicopter in this photo.

   a. subject   **b.** direct object   **c.** subject complement   **d.** object of another prepositional phrase

4. The symbol <u>over</u> the door is mysterious.

   a. subject   **b.** direct object   **c.** subject complement   **d.** object of another prepositional phrase

B. Fill in the blanks with a prepositional phrase that fits the context of the sentence.

1. The lamb fell in a hole _____ .

2. Darren's drawing is the one _____ .

3. The room behind that door _____ is a psychology lab.

4. Maria couldn't find the box _____ .

5. Ray got scared _____ .

C. Choose one topic and write about it in a paragraph that contains at least four sentences. In your paragraph, use prepositional phrases to modify at least one subject, at least one direct object, at least one subject complement, and at least one object of another prepositional phrase. You may choose your own topic. Possible topics:

looking for buried treasure	getting dressed up for a special event	dealing with very hot weather

_____

_____

_____

_____

© Houghton Mifflin Harcourt Publishing Company

Build Vocabulary

Compound Words

A. Write the words that make up each compound word.

1. lifetime   _____   _____
2. lifelike   _____   _____
3. candlelight   _____   _____
4. rainstorm   _____   _____
5. newspaper   _____   _____

B. Complete each sentence with the correct compound word from the box.

lifetime	candlelight	newspaper
lifelike	rainstorm	textbook
well-known	eye-catching	moonlight

1. The explorers explored the inside of the dark ancient tomb by _____ .
2. The pyramids looked magnificent in the _____ with twinkling stars overhead.
3. We rushed to get back into the house when we heard that there was a _____ coming.
4. I am reading a book about some of the _____ rulers of Egypt.
5. The colorful jacket that you're wearing is very _____ .

C. Choose four words from the box in Part B. Use each word in a sentence.

1. Word: _____

   _____

   _____

2. Word: _____

   _____

   _____

3. Word: _____

   _____

   _____

4. Word: _____

   _____

   _____

© Houghton Mifflin Harcourt Publishing Company

"Hatshepsut: The King Herself"

Unpack a Sentence

Use the guiding questions to help you unpack the sentences.

> "She even went as far as altering her appearance, wearing the ceremonial golden false beard of a pharaoh, which appears in paintings and statues of her."

1. Name one phrase central to understanding this sentence.

_____

_____

2. Why did she wear the beard of a pharaoh?

_____

_____

3. How do we know she wore the beard?

_____

_____

> "In her memorial temple on the bank of the Nile—itself one of the great monuments of Ancient Egypt—Hatshepsut is remembered in inscriptions and statues."

1. Name one phrase central to understanding this sentence.

_____

_____

2. What is a great monument of Ancient Egypt?

_____

_____

3. Where is the temple?

_____

_____

4. Why is the temple important?

_____

_____

© Houghton Mifflin Harcourt Publishing Company

Academic Vocabulary

A. Complete each sentence with the correct word from the box.

focus	focused

1. Cameron ignored the noise from the crowd and _____ on reaching the finish line.

focus	focused

2. If you can't find the answer in the first paragraph, _____ on a different paragraph.

focus	focused

3. Mr. Duane was so _____ on his work that he didn't see the giraffe walk by.

focus	focused

4. I'm able to _____ better when I study with my friends.

B. Read the passage and answer the questions.

The focus of Vivian's photography project was her hometown in France. She was focusing on French architecture. By using a special lens to focus her camera, she could take clear photos of buildings from a distance.

1. What is the focus of Vivian's project?

The focus of her project is _____.

2. What had she been focusing on?

She had been focusing on _____.

3. How was she able to take clear photos of buildings from a distance?

She used _____.

C. Use *focus* in a sentence describing a hobby or favorite activity.

_____

_____

_____

© Houghton Mifflin Harcourt Publishing Company

Collaborative Discussion Support

Use the outline below to help you summarize or retell the main ideas of the selection in your own words. Remember the most important idea is the one that can be supported by each of the other facts and details in the paragraph. Avoid including opinions or judgments; just describe the facts.

"Hatshepsut: The King Herself"

I. Introduction

Thesis Statement: _____

_____

II. Rise to Power

   A. _____

   _____

                      (Main idea # 1)

   B. _____

                      (Main idea # 2)

III. A Successful Reign

   A. _____

                      (Main idea # 3)

   B. _____

                      (Main idea # 4)

IV. Conclusion

_____

          (Restatement of the thesis/summary of aspects)

Rewrite the summary sentences in one paragraph. Add transition words and pronouns to make the paragraph flow.

Summary paragraph: _____

_____

_____

_____

_____

_____

© Houghton Mifflin Harcourt Publishing Company

Persuasive Speech

Hatshepsut: The King Herself

To evaluate your speech, use the Presenting a Speech Rubric available from your online Student Resources or from your teacher.

A. Plan

1. Plan the occasion and topic for a short speech Hatshepsut might give to her citizens.

   The occasion for this speech will be…

   _____

   _____

   Topic: What does Hatshepsut want to persuade her citizens to do or think?

   I want to…

   _____

   _____

2. What sources will you use to look up information about Hatshepsut's reign?

   _____

B. Prepare

A well-organized speech is easier to remember.

Introduction: What will be your opening line? *(Grab your listeners' attention.)*

_____

_____

_____

Important Points: What are your main points? What facts and details will you include?

1. _____

2. _____

3. _____

Conclusion: How will you end your speech? What do you want your listeners to remember?

_____

_____

_____

© Houghton Mifflin Harcourt Publishing Company

Build Vocabulary

Vocabulary Strategy: Latin Roots

civilization	civic	century	justice
centenarian	justify	justification	

A. Choose a word from the box to answer each question.

1. Which word describes someone's duty as a citizen? _____

2. Which word means "someone who has lived for a hundred years"? _____

3. Which word means "a period of 100 years"? _____

4. Which word means "an acceptable reason for doing something"? _____

5. Which word means "the process or result of applying laws fairly"? _____

B. Complete each sentence with a word from the box.

1. The history of Egyptian _____ has captured the interest of both scholars and ordinary people.

2. Even though he knew he was wrong, Frank tried for a full half hour to _____ his behavior.

3. It is your _____ duty to learn about the candidates running for office.

4. The Italian artist Michelangelo was born in the 15th _____ .

5. At 100 years old the _____ is still active and alert.

C. Choose five words from the box. Use each word in a sentence. Write the sentence in the space.

1. _____
   _____

2. _____
   _____

3. _____
   _____

4. _____
   _____

5. _____
   _____

© Houghton Mifflin Harcourt Publishing Company

Critical Vocabulary

A. Read the sentences below. Circle the definition of each underlined word. Remember that you can look up any unfamiliar words in the dictionary.

1. I proved that a woman could write a novel that was as deep and <u>compelling</u> as any novel written by a man—the truth of which is generally accepted today. *Compelling* means

   a. difficult and boring.   **b.** interesting and powerful.   **c.** long and heavy.

2. Your work certainly helped <u>achieve</u> that. *Achieve* means

   a. begin.   **b.** force.   **c.** accomplish.

3. Our next speaker will be someone <u>familiar</u> to many of you. *Familiar* means

   a. known.   **b.** appealing.   **c.** alien.

4. Clever inventions do not <u>guarantee</u> a peaceful existence. *Guarantee* means

   a. promise.   **b.** hurt.   **c.** make difficult.

5. We did many good things. I think that's the most <u>profound</u> thing we share. *Profound* means

   a. deep.   **b.** famous.   **c.** not relevant.

B. Choose a word from the box to complete each sentence.

compelling	achieve	familiar	guarantee	disguise	profound

1. I can _____ that you will be very popular at my house.

2. Abraham Lincoln's life story is very _____ .

3. I am working hard so I can _____ my goals.

4. The character in the play had to _____ himself in order to get through the city unnoticed.

5. The man expressed his _____ thanks for our help.

6. This street looks _____ . I must have been here before.

C. Choose three words from the box in Part B. Use each word in a sentence.

1. _____

   _____

2. _____

   _____

3. _____

   _____

© Houghton Mifflin Harcourt Publishing Company

Build Vocabulary

Expressions

A. Circle the correct answer.

1. What expression or idiom means "something that is done to achieve something else"?

   a. means to an end   **b.** lasting value

2. Which expression or idiom describes wanting to be viewed as important and worthy of consideration?

   a. to be taken seriously   **b.** no one was the wiser

3. What expression or idiom means "at a particular time in the past"?

   a. back then   **b.** means to an end

4. What expression or idiom describes people who are unaware of something?

   a. suffer the same fate   **b.** no one was the wiser

5. What expression or idiom means to "endure the same outcome"?

   a. no one was the wiser   **b.** suffer the same fate

around the globe   to be taken seriously   back when   no one was the wiser   means to an end

B. Complete each sentence with a phrase from the box.

1. _____ people had no cars, many rode horses.

2. Winning the science contest was just a _____ .

3. As a biologist studying climate change, Wayne had the opportunity to travel _____ .

4. Arlene was determined _____ even though no one had ever considered a woman for the position.

5. They had hacked into the company's computer system, but _____ .

C. Choose four phrases from the box. Use each phrase in a sentence.

1. _____
   _____

2. _____
   _____

3. _____
   _____

4. _____
   _____

© Houghton Mifflin Harcourt Publishing Company

Adjective Clauses with Relative Pronouns

A. **Decide whether you can combine the sentences as shown with "who," "whom," "whose," or none of the above. Circle the correct answer.**

1. They gave a medal to TJ. He stopped that fire.

   a. They gave a medal to TJ, who stopped that fire.

   b. They gave a medal to TJ, whom stopped that fire.

   c. They gave a medal to TJ, whose stopped that fire.

   d. None of the above

2. That's Chris's trombone. His dad gave it to him.

   a. That's Chris's trombone, who his dad gave to him.

   b. That's Chris's trombone, whom his dad gave to him.

   c. That's Chris's trombone, whose his dad gave to him.

   d. None of the above

3. I asked Pedro what I should do. His dog got sick last year.

   a. I asked Pedro, who dog got sick last year, what I should do.

   b. I asked Pedro, whom dog got sick last year, what I should do.

   c. I asked Pedro, whose dog got sick last year, what I should do.

   d. None of the above

4 Hyun-sook Choi runs a dog-walking business. I met her in the park.

   a. Hyun-sook Choi, who I met in the park, runs a dog-walking business.

   b. Hyun-sook Choi, whom I met in the park, runs a dog-walking business.

   c. Hyun-sook Choi, whose I met in the park, runs a dog-walking business.

   d. None of the above.

B. **Fill in the blank with a clause that fits the context of the sentence.**

1. Ximena, whose _____, saw her at the grocery store.

2. Mr. Chou, whose _____, visits him once a year.

3. The boy whom _____ is recovering.

4. This physicist, who _____, wants to find out why the laws of physics are what they are.

5. The nurse who _____ normally works the night shift.

© Houghton Mifflin Harcourt Publishing Company

Collaborative Discussion Support

Discuss the Purpose

Choose a character to analyze from "A Means to an End." Use the questions below to help you evaluate the character's motives.

Historical Figure

_____   _____
       Female Name   Male Name

1. List the reasons for the disguise.

- _____
- _____
- _____

2. What was the character's primary motivation? What did she most want to accomplish?

_____

3. What circumstances were preventing her from achieving her goal?

_____

4. What other means could she have taken to accomplish her goals?

_____

Academic Vocabulary

A. Complete each sentence with the correct word from the box.

perceive	perceptive

1. Animals can use different senses to _____ that an earthquake is coming before humans do.

perception	perceptive

2. Eric and Amy are writing a play. They want to share their _____ of the challenges that modern teenagers face.

perceptive	misperception

3. When Ross was far away, he thought he saw a castle in the distance, but when he came closer he realized his _____.

perception	perceptive

4. If I enjoy a story, it's often because the author is very _____ about what will interest a reader.

B. Complete each sentence.

1. One misperception I used to have is _____.

2. If I perceive that someone doesn't agree with me, I usually _____.

C. Think about sitting down to eat a delicious warm meal. Explain how at least three different senses help you to perceive your food.

_____

_____

_____

_____

_____

_____

_____

_____

_____

© Houghton Mifflin Harcourt Publishing Company

Staying on Task

Monitoring your comprehension while reading can help you to stay focused. Use these prompts to help you stay on task.

1. When and where does the story take place? Who are the main characters?

_____

_____

_____

2. What words or phrases do I not know? Can I use context clues, the art, and the dictionary to help me to understand this text?

_____

_____

_____

3. Based on the facts so far, what can I predict will happen next?

_____

_____

_____

4. Does the author use words or sentences in an interesting way? How does this influence the meaning?

_____

_____

_____

5. Is something confusing? What is it? Reread.

_____

_____

_____

6. Look for clues to solve the mystery.

_____

_____

_____

© Houghton Mifflin Harcourt Publishing Company

Critical Vocabulary

A. Read the sentences below. Circle the definition of each underlined word. Remember that you can look up any unfamiliar words in the dictionary.

1. The office was boarded up, and the plaque on the door was gone. *Plaque* means

   a. small metal or wood sign.   **b.** hanging bell.   **c.** door knocker.

2. Mr. Holmes's reputation is well-deserved. *Reputation* means

   a. dislike.   **b.** competition.   **c.** fame.

3. I was well aware that the directions were a ruse, a way of gathering information. *Ruse* means

   a. truth.   **b.** trick.   **c.** accident.

4. We watched in awe as a man climbed out of the opening. *Awe* means

   a. amazement.   **b.** disrespect.   **c.** happiness.

5. Thanks to you, Holmes, we finally got the notorious bank robber John Clay! *Notorious* means

   a. very last.   **b.** well-known for bad things.   **c.** completely unknown.

B. Choose a word from the box to complete each sentence.

eccentric	plaque	reputation	ruse
cellar	awe	notorious	imminent

1. There's a _____ on the wall that says Mark Twain lived here.

2. Edith and Steve go down to the _____ when there's a tornado warning.

3. There are signs that a volcanic eruption is _____.

4. That artist has a reputation for being _____ because she doesn't try to look like everyone else.

5. John has a _____ as a great goalkeeper.

6. Elizabeth's teammates watched in _____ as she made seven baskets in a row.

7. This _____ criminal will be in jail for many years.

8. Some girls disguised themselves as men as a _____ to be able to do things girls weren't allowed to do.

C. Choose three words from the box in Part B. Use each word in a sentence.

1. _____

2. _____

3. _____

© Houghton Mifflin Harcourt Publishing Company

Build Vocabulary

Context and Picture Clues

deserted	imminent	ruse	illicit
carriage	distracted	confounds	

A. Choose the correct word from the box to answer each question.

1. Which word means "a trick," or "an action intended to deceive someone"? _____

2. Which word describes an illegal activity? _____

3. Which word describes something that will happen very soon? _____

4. Which word means "distraught" or "mentally troubled"? _____

5. Which word means "a four-wheeled vehicle drawn by horses that carries people"? _____

B. Complete each sentence with the correct word from the box.

1. If you engage in _____ activities, you will probably end up in jail.

2. It _____ Carrie how effortlessly her sister solves difficult math problems.

3. If Greg doesn't study hard tonight he is in _____ danger of failing the test.

4. As a _____, my mother sent my father to the supermarket to get him out of the house while people gathered for his surprise birthday party.

C. Choose five words from the box. Use each word in a sentence.

1. _____
   _____

2. _____
   _____

3. _____
   _____

4. _____
   _____

5. _____
   _____

© Houghton Mifflin Harcourt Publishing Company

Homophones

A. Circle the correct homophone.

1. Which word means "a line where two pieces of cloth are joined together"?

   a. seam   **b.** seem

2. Which word means "lacking strength"?

   a. week   **b.** weak

3. Which word means "find out how heavy something is"?

   a. way   **b.** weigh

4. Which word means "a cylinder on which film, wire, or thread can be wound"?

   a. reel   **b.** real

5. Which word means "the number after three and before five"?

   a. four   **b.** for

B. Complete each sentence with the correct homonym.

1. Jason _____ out of sorts today. (seems, seams)

2. The sports team will head home in the _____. (morning, mourning)

3. There are many _____ to cook spaghetti sauce. (weighs, ways)

4. The pitcher _____ a fastball, which the hitter missed. (through, threw)

5. Kelly wound the wire around the _____. (reel, real)

real/reel	seem/seam	way/weigh
morning/mourning	through/threw	

C. Choose three homophone pairs from the box. Use each word in a sentence and underline the homophones.

1. _____

   _____

2. _____

   _____

3. _____

   _____

© Houghton Mifflin Harcourt Publishing Company

How English Works

Combinining Clauses in a Sentence

A. **Decide how to combine the sentences. Circle the correct answer.**

1. I saw a face at the window. It startled me.

   a. I saw a face at the window, which startled me.

   b. I saw a face at the window, that startled me.

   c. I saw a face at the window, when startled me.

   d. I saw a face at the window, where startled me.

2. Margaret worked with a tutor. The tutor helped her a lot.

   a. The tutor why Margaret worked with helped her a lot.

   b. The tutor that Margaret worked with helped her a lot.

   c. The tutor when Margaret worked with helped her a lot.

   d. The tutor where Margaret worked with helped her a lot.

3. The last book on the shelf is about chemistry. Rachel put it there.

   a. The last book on the shelf, why Rachel put there, is about chemistry.

   b. The last book on the shelf, where Rachel put there, is about chemistry.

   c. The last book on the shelf, when Rachel put there, is about chemistry.

   d. The last book on the shelf, that Rachel put there, is about chemistry.

4. The hospital closed. Sophie was born there.

   a. The hospital where Sophie was born closed.

   b. The hospital that Sophie was born closed.

   c. The hospital which Sophie was born closed.

   d. The hospital when Sophie was born closed.

B. **Fill in the blanks with a clause that fits the context of the sentence.**

1. The reason _____ is that she played a long soccer game today.

2. The painting was pink and orange, like the sky when _____ .

3. Mr. Ulrich's sword, that _____ , is definitely very old.

4. The cloud that _____ looked like a dragon to her.

5. My jacket, which _____ , is bright green.

© Houghton Mifflin Harcourt Publishing Company

Collaborative Discussion Support

Use the questions below to help guide and organize your thoughts about the crime mystery.

1. Were you able to solve the mystery before Holmes gave it away?

   a. If yes, what clues did you use to solve it?

   _____

   _____

   _____

   b. If no, what clues did you miss or misinterpret?

   _____

   _____

   _____

2. How did reading the story more than once help you to follow Sherlock Holmes' investigation? Which clues were more evident?

   _____

   _____

   _____

3. What conclusion did Holmes come to that surprised you?

   _____

   _____

   _____

4. What event in the story was most suspenseful?

   _____

   _____

   _____

5. If you had an opportunity to speak with Sherlock Holmes, what would you ask him about this mystery?

   _____

   _____

   _____

© Houghton Mifflin Harcourt Publishing Company

Analyze the Text Support

Use the questions below to help you summarize the mystery.

1. Who are the characters?

   _____

   _____

   _____

   _____

   _____

2. What are the events that make up the rising action?

   _____

   _____

   _____

   _____

   _____

   _____

3. What is the climax?

   _____

   _____

   _____

   _____

   _____

4. What is the resolution?

   _____

   _____

   _____

   _____

   _____

5. What is the falling action?

   _____

   _____

   _____

   _____

   _____

© Houghton Mifflin Harcourt Publishing Company

Prefixes *un–*, *dis–*, *il–*, and *ir–*

unimportant	irresponsible	irregular
disobey	disagree	unremarkable

A. Choose a word from the box to answer each question.

1. Which word means "not significant"? _____

2. Which word means "to have a different opinion"? _____

3. Which word means "to not follow rules "? _____

4. Which word means "dull, boring"? _____

5. Which word means "careless, negligent"? _____

B. Complete each sentence with a word from the box.

1. It's important never to _____ traffic signs.

2. Mai said it was _____ if I came to her party late as long as I came.

3. It is surprising that the restaurant is so expensive, especially given its _____ food.

4. My work schedule is unpredictable, and my hours are _____ .

5. It's _____ to just toss trash anywhere you want.

C. Choose three words from the box. Use each word in a sentence.

1. _____

_____

_____

2. _____

_____

_____

3. _____

_____

_____

© Houghton Mifflin Harcourt Publishing Company

Performance Task

Essay Main Ideas

A. Here is a list of the reading and podcast selections in this unit. Pick three of the selections and describe the main idea of each one you choose.

"School Daze"

"Eat 'Em Up"

from The Giver

"Lessons from the Perry Como Sundae Bar"

"Hatshepsut: The King Herself"

"A Means to an End"

"The Red-Headed League"

_____

_____

_____

B. Write three possible main ideas for your essay.

1. _____

_____

_____

_____

2. _____

_____

_____

_____

3. _____

_____

_____

_____

© Houghton Mifflin Harcourt Publishing Company

Plan Your Essay

Main Idea

Write your main idea. Remember, you can use a statement or a question. You may also include an interesting quote from one of the selections.

_____

_____

_____

Supporting Details

What details will support your main idea?

_____

_____

What evidence from the texts can you use?

_____

_____

What other sources can you use to find details?

_____

_____

Vocabulary

Are there any proper nouns that you may need to explain?

_____

_____

Text Features

What are some ideas for the title of your essay?

_____

_____

What subheads will you use in your essay? Remember, subheads are needed if your supporting details can be grouped together.

_____

_____

_____

© Houghton Mifflin Harcourt Publishing Company

Academic Vocabulary

A. Write an example of a task for each occupation.

Occupation	Task
Chef	
Teacher	
Veterinarian	
Firefighter	
Student	

B. Read the passage and answer the questions.

> Some neuroscientists have been experimenting with video games to help older adults improve mental fitness. As people get older, they are not usually able to multitask as well as younger people. Some experiments show that if older adults do something challenging, like learning a new language or maybe playing a video game with complex tasks, they can sharpen their brains.

1. What do many older people lose the ability to do well?

They may lose the ability to _____.

2. What kind of video games may help older people sharpen their brains?

Playing _____ may sharpen their brains.

C. Write a sentence explaining the things you do when you multitask.

_____

_____

_____

_____

_____

© Houghton Mifflin Harcourt Publishing Company

Finalize Your Plan

To evaluate your essay, use the Writing an Informative Essay Rubric available from your online Student Resources or from your teacher.

WRITING TOOLBOX

Elements of an Informative Essay

Opening Paragraph	Present your main idea. Include an interesting fact, question, or quotation.
Supporting Detail	Each paragraph should include a supporting detail to support your main idea. You may want to use subheads to group your ideas.
Conclusion	The conclusion should sum up how the details support your main idea. You may want to include a question to make the reader think.

A. Review the elements of an informative essay above. Describe the elements that you will include in your essay.

Opening Paragraph _____

_____

_____

Supporting Details _____

_____

_____

Conclusion _____

_____

_____

B. Write a brief summary of your essay.

_____

_____

_____

© Houghton Mifflin Harcourt Publishing Company

Vocabulary Review

Here are some of the words you learned in this unit. Choose words from this list and sort them into the categories below. There are many possible correct answers!

abnormal	familiar	litigator	reputation
achieve	feature	lure	ruse
asserted	focus	magician	shuffled
auditorium	genetic	miraculous	situation
candlelight	guarantee	morning	task
capacity	illicit	mourning	threw
carriage	imminent	notions	through
century	irregular	notorious	tones
civilization	irresponsible	nutrients	unremarkable
deck	justification	offense	vibrant
digest	justify	pedestrian	victorious
disguise	lifelike	perceive	volunteers
disobey	litigable	powerful	way
eccentric	litigate	profound	weigh
exception	litigation	prosperous	

Homophone Pairs

1. _____
   _____

2. _____
   _____

Words with Suffixes

1. _____
2. _____
3. _____
4. _____
5. _____

Words with Prefixes

1. _____
2. _____
3. _____
4. _____
5. _____

Nouns

1. _____
2. _____
3. _____
4. _____
5. _____

© Houghton Mifflin Harcourt Publishing Company

Easily Confused Words

A. Circle the correct word in each sentence. Use the context clues to help you decide.

1. I [infer, imply] from the grass stains on Mark's pants that he's been playing in the field.

2. Did you [here, hear] that howl?

3. Joanne's bike is better [then, than] mine.

4. My baby sister [ways, weighs] three kilograms.

B. Fill in the blanks with the correct word that fits the context of each sentence.

1. Her silence seemed to _____ that she disagreed.

2. Uh-oh, there's no _____ we'll get to the concert on time.

3. The truck slowed and _____ stopped.

4. If you come home before six, your uncle will be _____.

5. Al is way taller _____ me.

C. Write four sentences, one using *imply* or *infer*, one using *here* or *hear,* one using *then* or *than,* and one using *way* or *weigh.* Your sentences should demonstrate your understanding of the meaning of each word.

1. _____

_____

_____

_____

2. _____

_____

_____

_____

3. _____

_____

_____

_____

4. _____

_____

_____

_____

© Houghton Mifflin Harcourt Publishing Company

Nature at Work

Yet nature does nothing uselessly.

—Jules Verne, writer

What do you think of when you hear the word *nature*? You can make written or visual notes.

How far would you have to go to observe nature?

_____

_____

What kind of nature could you observe on the grounds of the school?

_____

_____

Where could you observe nature in your town?

_____

_____

What are some of the material things human beings get from nature?

_____

_____

What activities connect human beings with nature?

_____

_____

© Houghton Mifflin Harcourt Publishing Company

Build Vocabulary

Academic Vocabulary

As you work through Unit 3, look and listen for these words. Use them when you talk in class and in your writing. Write about your experiences using these words in the last column of the chart.

Word	Definition	Related Forms	My Experiences
affect	to influence or change something	effect, unaffected	
element	• one of the basic substances that cannot be split into simpler substances by using chemistry • a part or aspect of something	the elements, elementary	
ensure	to make sure or certain	insurance	
participate	to be active or involved in something	participant, participation	
specify	to state exactly or in detail what you want or need	specific, specifically	

© Houghton Mifflin Harcourt Publishing Company

Guess Which One?

Read page 103 of the Student Book to guide you in completing this task.

Use the chart to make notes for playing "Guess Which One?"

	Adjectives	Looks, Feels, Smells, Tastes, or Sounds Like...	Makes Me Think Of...
mountain path			
sun			
cloud			
crow			
ice cream			
other			

My three examples of figurative language:

_____

_____

_____

© Houghton Mifflin Harcourt Publishing Company

Collaborative Discussion Support

Use the graphic organizer below to compare and contrast the voices of the teen bloggers—
GoGirl in Unit 1 and the School Daze blogger in Unit 2—with the adult blogger in "Going Wild."
Make notes about word choices, mood, and tone.

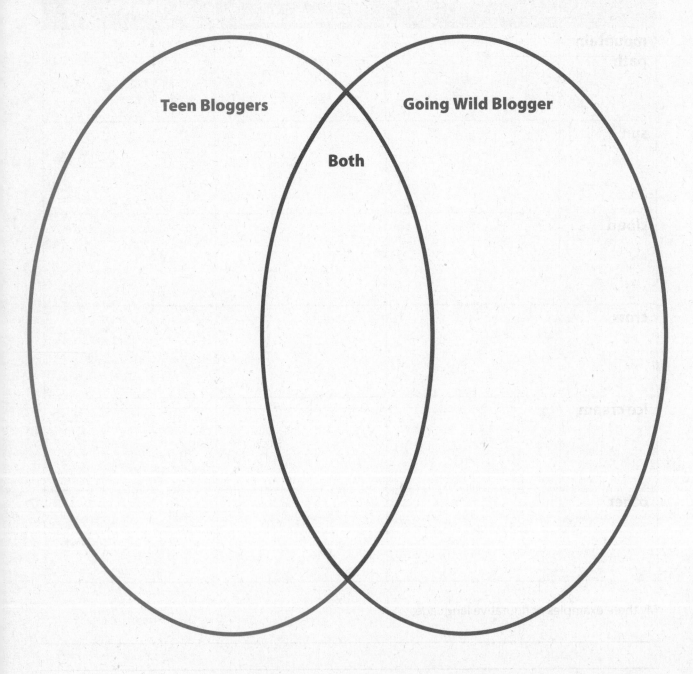

Teen Bloggers

Going Wild Blogger

Both

© Houghton Mifflin Harcourt Publishing Company

Critical Vocabulary

A. Read the sentences below from the blog "Going Wild." Circle the definition of each underlined word. Remember that you can look up any unfamiliar words in the dictionary.

1. Our research team has been <u>monitoring</u> the beavers' progress on their dam for many days. *Monitoring* means

    a. observing.   **b.** strengthening.   **c.** listing.

2. Beavers are mostly <u>nocturnal</u> and are just starting to work on the dam tonight. *Nocturnal* means

    a. active in the morning.   **b.** active at night.   **c.** active in the summer.

3. Beavers build their dams by <u>hauling</u> rocks, sticks, larger branches, and mud they dig up from the river's floor. *Hauling* means

    a. carrying.   **b.** jumping on.   **c.** organizing.

4. Thanks to teeth that always remain sharp, beavers can <u>gnaw</u> through trees of every size. *Gnaw* means

    a. go.   **b.** see.   **c.** chew.

B. Choose a word from the box to complete each sentence.

monitoring	binoculars	nocturnal	hauling	gnaw	elaborate

1. Beavers don't study engineering, but the dams they build are very _____.
2. Nothing makes the little mouse happier than to _____ on a nice piece of cheese.
3. Cats are _____, which is why they sleep so much during the day.
4. Mr. Mac takes his _____ when he goes bird watching.

C. Choose three words from the box in Part B. Use each word in a sentence.

1. _____

   _____

2. _____

   _____

3. _____

   _____

© Houghton Mifflin Harcourt Publishing Company

Write On! Support

Use this page to organize your ideas for the Write On! assignment on page 106 of the Student Book.

Animals I might like to write about			
squirrel	turtle	Monarch butterfly	bumblebee

Think about the animals and why you might like to write about each of them. Then circle the one you chose to write about.

What I know about _____,

_____

_____

_____

_____

_____

_____

Look for information about the animal you have chosen in your school library or online.

New information

_____

_____

_____

_____

_____

_____

© Houghton Mifflin Harcourt Publishing Company

Performance Task

Writing a Blog

To evaluate your blog, use the Blog Rubric available from your online Student Resources or from your teacher.

Choose a Design

Use these questions to help you choose a design for your blog.

1. What words would I use to describe the look I would like to have? Circle two or three. Add your own words in the spaces provided.

   - beautiful
   - fun
   - creative
   - cheerful

   - edgy
   - clean
   - festive
   - dark

   - different
   - bold
   - _____
   - _____

2. What colors would give me the look I want? Circle as many as you like.

   - bright red
   - dark red
   - yellow
   - orange
   - light brown
   - dark brown

   - dark blue
   - light blue
   - bright blue
   - lavender
   - purple
   - pink

   - dark green
   - bright green
   - pale green
   - black
   - _____
   - _____

3. What features would I like?

   - favorite links
   - blog archive

   - photo gallery
   - registration

   - _____
   - _____

© Houghton Mifflin Harcourt Publishing Company

Vocabulary Strategy: Reference Aids (Glossary)

bullet	a large black dot used to mark each item in a list
font	a specific typeface with a certain size and style
layout	the arrangement of words and images on a page
sidebar	on a text or web page, a single column to the left or right of the main part of the page
template	a preset layout (as for a blog) that can be adapted to fit many users
upload	to move or copy a computer file from one place to another

A. Choose a word from the Glossary to answer each question.

1. Where does a web page often list different sections of the website? _____

2. Which word describes how you would copy a photo from your camera onto a blog page?

_____

3. What is the word for the arrangement of text and pictures on a page? _____

B. Complete each sentence with a word from the Glossary.

1. Daniel looked at over 100 designs before choosing the "Adventure" _____ for his blog.

2. At first, Doreen chose the Jokerman _____ for her blog posts, but the letters were too weird, so she changed to Arial.

3. Putting a _____ next to each link on the "Visit My Friends" list made Julia's blog page easier to read.

C. Choose two words from the glossary. Use each word in a sentence. Write the sentences in the space.

1. _____

_____

2. _____

_____

© Houghton Mifflin Harcourt Publishing Company

Adverbs

A. Decide if the underlined word is an adverb modifying a verb, an adjective, or another adverb, or if it is not an adverb.

1. Those flowers look <u>very</u> familiar.

    a. adverb modifying a verb
    b. adverb modifying an adjective
    c. adverb modifying an adverb
    d. not an adverb

2. The fox cubs were <u>quite</u> happily chasing each other.

    a. adverb modifying a verb
    b. adverb modifying an adjective
    c. adverb modifying an adverb
    d. not an adverb

3. I <u>always</u> want to go someplace new!

    a. adverb modifying a verb
    b. adverb modifying an adjective
    c. adverb modifying an adverb
    d. not an adverb

4. We were really afraid <u>of</u> the bees, but they ignored us.

    a. adverb modifying a verb
    b. adverb modifying an adjective
    c. adverb modifying an adverb
    d. not an adverb

B. Fill in the blanks with an adverb that fits.

1. Wild turkeys _____ travel in large groups.

2. She was _____ reluctantly willing to watch the puppies being born.

3. The mother deer _____ nudged her fawn.

4. Speak _____ so you don't disturb the animals.

5. The hike was _____ difficult.

C. Choose one topic and write a paragraph about it. Include at least one frequency adverb, and use adverbs to modify at least one verb, at least one adjective, and at least one other adverb. Possible topics:

taking care of a houseplant or garden	learning a dance	going on rides at a fair or theme park

_____

_____

_____

_____

© Houghton Mifflin Harcourt Publishing Company

Cause/Effect

Answer the questions about *Hawks and Beavers*.

1. What are the kids doing their report about?

2. How do sharp talons help the falcon?

3. What does the tooth in the beak of the falcon do?

4. What was the effect of using the pesticide DDT on the birds of prey?

5. How was the dam created?

6. What was the cause of the flooding in the surrounding area?

7. What was the effect of this?

Compare and Contrast

Think about the video you have just seen. Compare and contrast it with "Going Wild."

1. What common topic do the video and the blog share?

2. How are the video and the blog different?

3. What is the most interesting thing you have learned in the video or the blog?

© Houghton Mifflin Harcourt Publishing Company

Build Vocabulary

UNIT 3

Critical Vocabulary

A. Circle four words in the Word Bank that you want to know more about.

Word Bank

bird of prey	capture	raptor	ensure	boundaries	impacted	environment
talons	pesticide	elements	conservation	borders	ecosystem	

B. Watch the video *Hawks and Beavers* again and listen for the words. Complete the activity.

1. Word: _____

What I think it means: _____

What it means: _____

2. Word: _____

What I think it means: _____

What it means: _____

3. Word: _____

What I think it means: _____

What it means: _____

4. Word: _____

What I think it means: _____

What it means: _____

C. Choose three words that you wrote in Part B. Write a sentence using each word.

1. _____

_____

2. _____

_____

3. _____

_____

© Houghton Mifflin Harcourt Publishing Company

USE WITH LESSON 5.3   **111**

Academic Vocabulary

affected	effect	unaffected

A. Choose the word from the box that best completes each sentence.

1. Green tea always has a calming _____ on me.

2. Philip's house is on a hill so it was _____ by the flooding.

3. When Julianna tripped, it _____ the outcome of the race.

B. Read the passage and answer the questions.

People who live near the ocean often enjoy swimming, barbecues, and watching the sun set over the water, but the ocean can have a negative effect on their daily lives too. At high tide, the seawater sometimes floods the streets and gets into the city's water supply. This affects the quality of the drinking water. The beach residents are worried about climate change for this reason, but people who live inland are unaffected by the tides, and some of them are less concerned about climate.

1. What is one way the ocean can have a positive effect on people's lives?

People who live near the ocean _____

_____

2. How does the flooding affect the drinking water?

The seawater _____ and gets into the city's water supply.

3. Why are people who live inland less concerned about climate change?

People who live inland _____.

C. Using a form of the verb *affect*, write a sentence about how the weather affects the way you feel.

_____

_____

_____

© Houghton Mifflin Harcourt Publishing Company

Collaborative Discussion Support

Choose one of the haikus in the selection. Write it in the first box. Then make notes about what you hear and see in the haiku in each of the other boxes.

haiku

Structure

What does each line contribute to the poem?

first line	second line	third line

Language

figurative language	sound techniques

© Houghton Mifflin Harcourt Publishing Company

Critical Vocabulary

A. Read the sentences below. Circle the definition of each underlined word. Remember that you can look up any unfamiliar words in the dictionary.

1. I give permission for this slow spring rain to soak the violet beds. *Soak* means

   a. thoroughly wet. **b.** thoroughly roast. **c.** tightly pack.

2. In a misty rain, a butterfly is riding the tail of a cow. *Misty* means

   a. sunny. **b.** foggy. **c.** heavy.

3. Past the window, a solitary snowflake spins furiously. *Solitary* means

   a. pretty. **b.** white. **c.** single.

4. Is there some design in these deep random raindrops drying in the dust? *Random* means

   a. arranged. **b.** unplanned. **c.** gigantic.

B. Choose a word from the box to complete each sentence.

soak	misty	barnyard	pane	solitary	random

1. The strong wind had broken one _____ of the kitchen window.

2. The cat waited in the _____ while Eli milked the cows, hoping for a bit of fresh milk.

3. The teacher looks around the class and calls on a student at _____.

4. Maureen looked out the window and noticed a _____ sunflower growing in the middle of the lawn.

C. Choose three words from the box in Part B. Use each word in a sentence.

1. _____

   _____

2. _____

   _____

3. _____

   _____

© Houghton Mifflin Harcourt Publishing Company

Analyzing Text

Use the boxes below to answer the questions on p. 113 of the Student Book.

| Interpret
lines 19–21	

| Summarize
lines 28–30	

| Compare
all of the poems	

| Analyze Theme
of all of the poems	

© Houghton Mifflin Harcourt Publishing Company

Write a Haiku

Use this pattern to help you write your haiku. Follow the Performance Task directions on page 113 of the Student Book.

Line 1: 5 syllables Create a simple image, perhaps a setting you will put the rest of the haiku into.	_____ _____ _____ _____ _____ _____
Line 2: 7 syllables Put an animal, a plant, another natural object into the setting you have created in the first line. Use descriptive language.	_____ _____ _____ _____ _____ _____
Line 3: 5 syllables Finish your haiku with a slight twist or observation.	_____ _____ _____ _____ _____ _____

© Houghton Mifflin Harcourt Publishing Company

Build Vocabulary

Figurative Language

Figurative language appeals to the reader's senses and imagination. Identify the correct literary devices and words below.

A. Circle the correct answer.

1. Which is an example of a metaphor?

   a. The sea sleeps on a bed of stars.

   b. A snowflake spins furiously.

2. Which is an example of personification?

   a. A little dog barks.

   b. Every sand grain hears the snake crawling.

3. Which is an example of figurative language?

   a. The wind whispered in the trees.

   b. The wind in the trees made the branches move.

swallow	sleeping	whisper	roaring	hear

B. Complete each sentence with a word from the box.

1. The _____ of the river rapids grew deafening as we got closer.

2. Each fall, the maple tree's dry leaves _____ in the wind.

3. In winter, the cornfields lie _____ under a blanket of snow.

4. In springtime, the earth can _____ the clamor of sprouts bursting up to greet the sun.

5. Each morning of our camping trip, we watched dawn _____ the night.

C. Choose three words from the box. Use each word to describe something using figurative language. Use at least one metaphor, one simile, and one use of personification.

1. _____

   _____

2. _____

   _____

3. _____

   _____

© Houghton Mifflin Harcourt Publishing Company

Setting a Purpose

Use this KWL chart to help you set a purpose for listening to the podcast a second time. What do you know now, and what questions do you have? You will fill out the third column after you have listened to the podcast.

K	W	L
What I *Know*	**What I *Want* to Learn**	**What I Have *Learned***

© Houghton Mifflin Harcourt Publishing Company

Build Vocabulary

Critical Vocabulary

A. Read the sentences below with words from "Dolphins Recognize the Calls of Long-Lost Friends." Circle the definition of each underlined word. Remember that you can look up any unfamiliar words in the dictionary.

1. It's not a secret that humans have an abiding fascination with dolphins. *Abiding* means

   a. direct.   **b.** continuing.   **c.** confusing.

2. Bruck studied dolphins who were housed in research facilities across the U.S. *Facilities* means

   a. centers.   **b.** hospitals.   **c.** lakes.

3. When the dolphins heard a familiar whistle, they would swim eagerly towards the speaker. *Eagerly* means

   a. tragically.   **b.** awkwardly.   **c.** excitedly.

4. Janet Mann has studied dolphin behavior for decades. *Decades* means

   a. tens of years.   **b.** weeks.   **c.** thousands of years.

B. Choose a word from the box to complete each sentence.

abiding	generates	acquainted	facilities	eagerly	decades

1. The movie actor _____ crowds wherever he goes.

2. Angela looked at the board _____ to see if she had made the volleyball team.

3. During the first week of school, I try to get _____ with my new classmates.

4. Robert's uncle lived in the same house for two _____ .

C. Choose three words from the box in Part B. Use each word in a sentence.

1. _____
   _____

2. _____
   _____

3. _____
   _____

© Houghton Mifflin Harcourt Publishing Company

Adverbs

A. Decide if the underlined adverb is an intensifier, a regular comparative/superlative adverb, an irregular adverb, or a negative adverb. Circle the correct answer.

1. The cheetah runs the <u>fastest</u> of all animals.

    a. intensifier   **b.** regular comparative/superlative adverb   **c.** irregular adverb   **d.** negative

2. The boys stood <u>very</u> quietly as the herd of deer approached.

    a. intensifier   **b.** regular comparative/superlative adverb   **c.** irregular adverb   **d.** negative

3. I <u>never</u> saw them again.

    a. intensifier   **b.** regular comparative/superlative adverb   **c.** irregular adverb   **d.** negative

4. The yellow-throated canary sings the <u>best</u> of all.

    a. intensifier   **b.** regular comparative/superlative adverb   **c.** irregular adverb   **d.** negative

B. Fill in the blanks with an adverb that fits. Use the type of adverb shown in parentheses.

1. The teacher was _____ proud of the animal drawings we made. (intensifier)

2. Some guides listen _____ than others. (regular comparative/superlative adverb)

3. Miguel tried _____ than anyone else to find the mushrooms.
    (regular comparative/superlative adverb)

4. Alicia trains parrots _____ than anyone else. (irregular adverb)

5. She does _____ have any dogs of her own. (negative)

C. Choose one topic and write four sentences about it. Include at least one intensifier, one regular comparative/superlative adverb, one irregular adverb, and one negative adverb in your paragraph. You may choose your own topic. Possible topics:

winning a game	giving a gift to someone	your favorite animal

1. _____
    _____

2. _____
    _____

3. _____
    _____

4. _____
    _____

© Houghton Mifflin Harcourt Publishing Company

Collaborative Discussion Support

Use this page to make notes about your experience listening to the podcast.

What questions did I have before I listened?

_____
_____
_____
_____
_____

Which questions were answered?

_____
_____
_____
_____
_____

What questions did I think of while I was listening?

_____
_____
_____
_____
_____

What could I do to find answers to my unanswered questions?

_____
_____
_____
_____
_____

Use the information in this chart for the Collaborative Discussion from Student Book page 115.

© Houghton Mifflin Harcourt Publishing Company

Academic Vocabulary

A. Circle the correct answer.

1. Which of the following is not one of the elements on the table we study in chemistry?

   iron   helium   oxygen   sunlight   carbon

2. Which of the following is not an element of fiction?

   plot   setting   thunder   character   theme

3. Which of the following is not one of the elements that are forces of nature?

   rain   building   wind   lightning   thunder

B. Read the passage and answer the questions.

> In the United States, everyone has the right to a free elementary education. The main elements of this education include language, social studies, science, and math. In science class, students are introduced to the chemical elements on the periodic table. They study the weather and how the elements cause metal to rust, rocks to erode, and paint to peel off of walls.

1. What does everyone have a right to in the United States?

   Everyone has the right to _____.

2. What are the main elements of this education?

   The main elements of this education include _____.

3. What are students introduced to in science?

   Students are introduced to _____.

4. What do elements of weather do?

   The elements cause _____.

C. Write a sentence using *element* about the element of weather that you like most and why you like it.

_____

_____

_____

_____

_____

© Houghton Mifflin Harcourt Publishing Company

Build Vocabulary

UNIT 3

Critical Vocabulary

A. Read the sentences below. Circle the definition of each underlined word from the selection "Salt, Sand, and Gold." Remember that you can look up any unfamiliar words in the dictionary.

1. There are elements in nature that humans must have in order to survive, and sometimes these <u>vital</u> elements are not easily or locally obtained. *Vital* means

   a. necessary.   **b.** minor.   **c.** additional.

2. Because life depends on it, one of the most important jobs humans have is to seek and <u>procure</u> these vital elements. *Procure* means

   a. maintain.   **b.** sell.   **c.** get.

3. People need water, and the local environment does not supply enough of it. <u>Therefore</u> people must figure out a way to bring it from where it exists. *Therefore* means

   a. whether.   **b.** for that reason.   **c.** in spite of.

4. If the trackers make a mistake, both the men and the camels could die of <u>thirst</u>. *Thirst* means

   a. high blood pressure.   **b.** weak knees.   **c.** the need to drink liquid.

B. Choose a word from the box to complete each sentence.

vital	procure	therefore	route	precipitation	thirst

1. We're trying to decide whether to take the _____ that goes by the library or the one that goes under the train track.

2. The parents organization is working to _____ soccer shoes for the girls team.

3. In New England, most _____ in the winter comes as snow or freezing rain.

4. The Amazon rainforest is a _____ source of oxygen for the planet.

C. Choose three words from the box in Part B. Use each word in a sentence.

1. _____

   _____

2. _____

   _____

3. _____

   _____

© Houghton Mifflin Harcourt Publishing Company

USE WITH LESSON 12.3 **123**

Collaborative Discussion Support

Cause and Effect

Use this chart to identify cause-and-effect relationships on the first page of "Salt, Sand, and Gold." Use the signal words to help you identify the relationship.

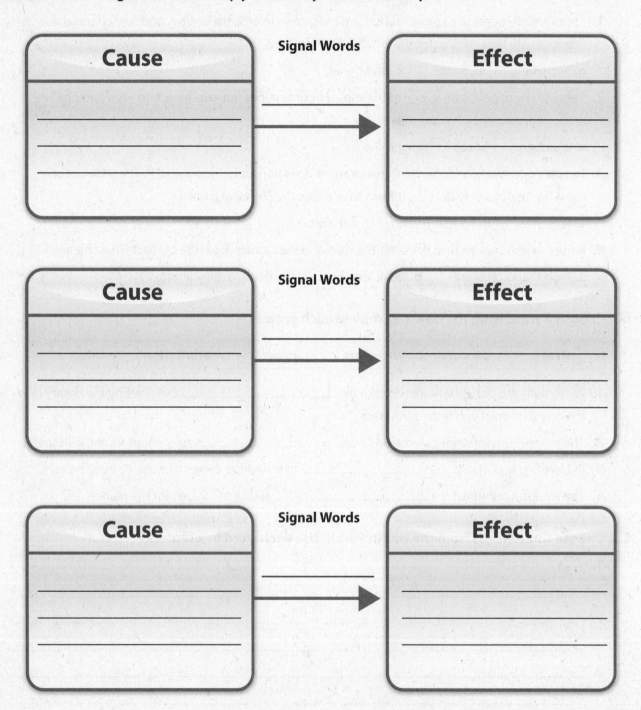

USE WITH STUDENT BOOK pp. 117 AND 121

© Houghton Mifflin Harcourt Publishing Company

"Salt, Sand, and Gold"

Write On!

Use this organizer to help you make notes about what you would need to pack for a trip across the Sahara, from the salt mines to Timbuktu.

What would you need to protect yourself from the sun?

_____

_____

_____

_____

What foods could you take that wouldn't spoil, wouldn't require water for cooking, and wouldn't make you thirsty?

_____

_____

_____

What could you use to carry water for yourself and your camel that you could refill and that wouldn't be too heavy?

_____

_____

_____

What kind of shoes would you take that would be comfortable in the heat and that you could walk long distances in?

_____

_____

_____

What else would you take that could come in handy?

_____

_____

_____

_____

© Houghton Mifflin Harcourt Publishing Company

Build Vocabulary

Antonyms

A. **For each sentence, choose the word below which is an *antonym* of the underlined word.**

1. Lost in the forest for two weeks, the women were able to <u>survive</u> by eating nuts and berries.

   a. perish   **b.** endure

2. Saving the rainforest is <u>vital</u> to ensure the well-being of the Earth.

   a. critical   **b.** unnecessary

3. The region's climate is one of <u>erratic</u> rainfall, where some months are dry and others wet.

   a. unpredictable   **b.** regular

4. The Gobi desert is <u>vast</u>, extending over an area more than three times as large as California.

   a. minute   **b.** enormous

5. Plant life is <u>abundant</u> in the rain forest, which has over 2500 species of vines.

   a. plentiful   **b.** scarce

B. **Complete each sentence with an antonym.**

1. The opposite of *vast* is _____ .

2. The opposite of *scarce* is _____ .

3. The opposite of *valuable* is _____ .

4. The opposite of *erratic* is _____ .

5. The opposite of *vital* is _____ .

C. **Choose two antonym pairs from your answers to activity B. Use each word in a sentence. Underline the antonyms.**

1. Antonyms: _____ and _____

   _____

   _____

   _____

2. Antonyms: _____ and _____

   _____

   _____

   _____

© Houghton Mifflin Harcourt Publishing Company

Critical Vocabulary

A. Read the sentences below. Circle the definition of each underlined word from "Alfred Wegener's Wild Idea" in the Student Book. Remember that you can look up any unfamiliar words in the dictionary.

1. One scientist proposed the idea that there had once been one large southern continent, but no one pursued the idea further. *Pursued* means

   a. signaled.   **b.** followed.   **c.** found.

2. Wegener found more evidence of similar organisms on both sides of the Atlantic, from worms to ferns to large animals. *Organisms* means

   a. mammals.   **b.** large trees.   **c.** living things.

3. Wegener was convinced that his idea of "continental displacement" was correct and began to publicize it. *Displacement* means

   a. movement.   **b.** neighbors.   **c.** disagreement.

4. The plates move, floating on a sea of molten rock called the "asthenosphere." *Molten* means

   a. melted.   **b.** leftover.   **c.** supporting.

B. Choose a word from the box to complete each sentence.

meteorology	pursued	organisms	displacement	drift	molten

1. If there is no wind to fill the sails, a sailboat can _____ off course.

2. We could see a little _____ lava flowing out of the volcano.

3. Some _____ are so tiny that you need a microscope to see them.

4. Ali loves watching the weather report on television and wants to study _____ in college.

C. Choose three words from the box in Part B. Use each word in a sentence.

1. _____

   _____

2. _____

   _____

3. _____

   _____

© Houghton Mifflin Harcourt Publishing Company

Prepositional Phrase

A. Decide whether the underlined phrase is a prepositional phrase of place, time, manner, or cause.

1. The branches swayed <u>above my head</u>.

   a. place   **b.** time   **c.** manner   **d.** cause

2. The cat attacked <u>with its sharp claws</u>.

   a. place   **b.** time   **c.** manner   **d.** cause

3. I couldn't see <u>because of the fog</u>.

   a. place   **b.** time   **c.** manner   **d.** cause

4. The woodpeckers start hammering <u>at dawn</u>.

   a. place   **b.** time   **c.** manner   **d.** cause

B. Fill in the blanks with a prepositional phrase that fits. Use the type of prepositional phrase shown in parentheses.

1. Khoury missed the trip _____. (cause)

2. The rosebush protects itself _____. (manner)

3. My dog eats _____. (place)

4. The cats were sleeping _____. (place)

5. Cecelia's goats have been eating grass _____. (time)

C. Choose one topic and write four sentences about it. Use prepositional phrases of place, time, manner, and cause. You may choose your own topic. Possible topics:

doing something nice for a friend	keeping in touch with someone far away	decorating a room

1. _____

   _____

2. _____

   _____

3. _____

   _____

4. _____

   _____

© Houghton Mifflin Harcourt Publishing Company

Build Vocabulary

Specialized Vocabulary

meteorology	organism	plate tectonics	fossils	geological

A. Choose the correct word from the box to answer each question.

1. Which term refers to huge masses of earth that move and shift? _____
2. Which word refers to the study of the earth? _____
3. Which word means "the remains and imprints of old life forms"? _____
4. Which word means an individual living thing? _____
5. Which word refers to the study of the weather? _____

B. Complete each sentence with the correct word from the box in Part A.

1. The human body is a complex _____.
2. At the natural history museum, we saw a _____ showing the imprint of an extinct fish.
3. _____ studies tell us that some rocks start out as mud, while other begin as liquids melted by extremely high temperatures.

C. Choose two words from the box. Use each word in a sentence.

1. _____
   _____
   _____
   _____

2. _____
   _____
   _____
   _____

© Houghton Mifflin Harcourt Publishing Company

USE WITH STUDENT BOOK pp. 123–125   USE WITH LESSON 15.3   **129**

Collaborative Discussion Support

Use the cluster diagram to make notes about Alfred Wegener's character traits. Cite lines from the text to support your observations.

curious

creative

Alfred Wegener

thorough

persistent

confident

© Houghton Mifflin Harcourt Publishing Company

Speaking Activity

To evaluate your speech, use the Presenting a Speech Rubric available from your online Student Resources or from your teacher. Follow the Performance Task directions on page 126 of the Student Book.

Plan

Use this section to organize your ideas for your speech as Alfred Wegener.

How did you think of your theory?

_____
_____
_____
_____

What did you do to research your theory?

_____
_____
_____
_____

Why do you think your theory is right?

_____
_____
_____
_____

Present

Use this section to organize your presentation.

Stage manager: _____

Cast: _____

Moderator: _____

Alfred Wegener: _____

Questioners: _____

Timer: _____

Props: _____

© Houghton Mifflin Harcourt Publishing Company

Academic Vocabulary

A. Read the passage and answer the questions.

> To ensure that everyone will receive payment for damages caused by car accidents, the legislature made a law that requires all drivers to have insurance. Car insurance might cost differently depending on things like the driver's age, location, type of car, and driving record.

1. Why did the legislature make a law?

The legislature made a law to ensure _____

_____.

2. What does the law require drivers to do?

The law requires all drivers _____

_____.

3. Why might the cost of car insurance change for different people? The cost of car insurance

depends on things like _____

_____.

B. Complete the sentences.

1. In order to protect our planet, we must ensure that _____.

2. When writing a report, ensure that each idea is supported by _____.

3. Dental insurance helps people by _____.

C. Using the word *ensure,* write a sentence about how you can ensure that your writing is organized and logical.

_____

_____

_____

_____

_____

_____

_____

_____

© Houghton Mifflin Harcourt Publishing Company

Vocabulary Strategy: Word Origins

A. Answer the questions about the dictionary entry.

Dictionary Entry

> **ge·ol·o·gy** (jē-ŏl⊥ə-jē) *n.* the scientific study of the origin, history, and structure of the earth [Greek *geō-*, earth+ Greek *-logiā*, speech]

1. What part of speech is *geology*? _____

2. What is the language of origin for *geology*? _____

3. What does the Greek root *geō-* mean? _____

4. What does the Greek root *-logiā* mean? _____

5. How would you put these two roots together to come up with a meaning for *geology*?

_____

Word	Word Origin	Words of Origin	Definition
geology	Greek	*geo + logia*	*science of earth*
Pangaea	Greek	*pan + gaea*	*supercontinent*
meteorology	Greek	*meteōron + logos*	*science of weather*
asthenosphere	Greek	*asthenēs + sphaira*	*sea of molten rock*
tectonic	Greek	*tektōn*	*of a geological structure*

B. Look at the box the with word origins and original meanings. Complete each sentence with the correct word from the box.

1. The science of _____ tells us that heat under the earth's surface changes limestone into marble.

2. Below the solid surface of the earth is a sea of molten rock called the _____.

3. The continents are the upper part of _____ plates on which the surface of earth "floats."

4. Scientists now believe that Europe and America were once a _____ or single supercontinent.

5. Many of these ideas were initially proposed by Alfred Wegener, who first studied _____, the science of weather.

C. Write two sentences that each use a word from Part B.

1. _____

2. _____

© Houghton Mifflin Harcourt Publishing Company

Onomatopoeia

A. **Circle the correct answer.**

1. Which is an example of something that makes a clicking sound?

   a. a lamp switch   **b.** a person's breath

2. Which word means a dull sound, as of a heavy object hitting the floor?

   a. thud   **b.** creak

3. Which is an example of something that might screech?

   a. a screaming child   **b.** an explosion

4. Which word means a squeaking sound, like a step on an old floorboard?

   a. thud   **b.** creak

5. Which is an example of something that would make a rumbling sound?

   a. a train whistle   **b.** distant thunder

clicking	thud	creak	tinkle	rumbling	screech

B. **Complete each sentence with a word from the box.**

1. On the porch of the lodge, Elaine heard the _____ of the sleigh bells as the sled came near.

2. Joe dropped the heavy box on the floor with a _____.

3. We could hear the swaying aspen trees _____ in the wind.

4. The _____ of the crickets was surprisingly loud on the lawn after dark.

5. The _____ owl is known for its shrill, high-pitched cry.

C. **Choose three words from the box. Use each word in a sentence.**

1. _____

   _____

2. _____

   _____

3. _____

   _____

© Houghton Mifflin Harcourt Publishing Company

Critical Vocabulary

A. Read the sentences below. Circle the definition of each underlined word. Remember that you can look up any unfamiliar words in the dictionary.

1. I held my breath in frightened <u>anticipation</u>. *Anticipation* means

   a. expectation. **b.** shaking. **c.** prediction.

2. I screamed, my voice getting lost in the <u>din</u>. *Din* means

   a. water puddles. **b.** loud, continuous noise. **c.** crumbling wall.

3. I opened my eyes and saw one of Ronnie's work boots <u>thud</u> against my side. *Thud* means

   a. stick. **b.** press. **c.** bang.

4. It felt like a never-ending stream of <u>chaos</u>. *Chaos* means

   a. doubt. **b.** worries. **c.** complete confusion.

B. Choose a word from the box to complete each sentence.

locomotive	anticipation	din	battered	thud	chaos

1. When the team got a last-minute touchdown, the _____ in the stadium caused many people to cover their ears.

2. The hurricane winds _____ the palm trees along the coast.

3. Trains were originally pulled by a _____ and ended with a caboose.

4. The mayor announced that schools will be closed tomorrow in _____ of heavy snow and wind.

C. Choose three words from the box in Part B. Use each word in a sentence.

1. _____

_____

2. _____

_____

3. _____

_____

Adverb Clauses

A. Decide whether the underlined adverb clause is an adverb clause of place, time, cause and effect, or none of the above. Circle the correct answer.

1. The boys left <u>because they wanted to play soccer</u>.

   a. place   **b.** time   **c.** cause and effect   **d.** none of the above

2. We'll go to the beach <u>unless it rains</u>.

   a. place   **b.** time   **c.** cause and effect   **d.** none of the above

3. I'll meet you <u>after I water the garden</u>.

   a. place   **b.** time   **c.** cause and effect   **d.** none of the above

4. Mr. Martinez travels <u>wherever there are parrots</u>.

   a. place   **b.** time   **c.** cause and effect   **d.** none of the above

B. Fill in the blank with a clause that fits the context of the sentence.

1. The park is crowded because _____!

2. Mom feeds the dog before _____.

3. If _____, we'll go swimming in the ocean.

4. I could be happy wherever _____.

5. We have to leave before dawn so that _____.

C. Choose one topic and write four sentences about it. Use adverb clauses of place, time, and cause and effect in each sentence. Be sure to use one of each type; place, time, and cause and effect. You may choose your own topic. Possible topics:

a water balloon fight	space exploration	describe how you like to dress

1. _____

   _____

2. _____

   _____

3. _____

   _____

4. _____

   _____

© Houghton Mifflin Harcourt Publishing Company

Academic Vocabulary

A. Complete each sentence with the correct word from the box.

participate	participant	participation

1. Mr. Polgreen asked for volunteers to _____ in a special project.

2. The principal changed the rules of the competition to encourage greater _____.

3. Lindiwe was excited to be a _____ in the Youth Assembly at the United Nations representing South Africa.

4. If more students _____ in the chess club, we can organize a tournament.

B. Complete each sentence.

1. Class participation means doing things like _____.

2. If I could participate in any sport, I would choose _____ because _____
   _____.

C. Write a sentence about an activity or organization you think more people should participate in. Use one of the words from the box.

_____

_____

_____

_____

_____

_____

_____

_____

© Houghton Mifflin Harcourt Publishing Company

Build Vocabulary

Critical Vocabulary

A. Read the sentences below. Circle the definition of each underlined word. Remember that you can look up any unfamiliar words in the dictionary.

1. We made snares to catch birds. *Snares* means

   a. chains.　　**b.** butterfly nets.　　**c.** traps.

2. At dawn, the storm ended. *Dawn* means

   a. sunset.　　**b.** sunrise.　　**c.** midnight.

3. Soon Fritz and I returned to the ship for more supplies. *Supplies* means

   a. materials.　　**b.** relatives.　　**c.** sheep.

4. The bamboo will make an excellent rope ladder. *Ladder* means

   a. movable stairs.　　**b.** cooking basket.　　**c.** net.

B. Choose a word from the box to complete each sentence.

withstand	dawn	supplies	storage	ladder	snares

1. Some cheese is kept in _____ in caves for several years before it is eaten.

2. A fire engine has a very tall _____ so the firefighters can reach the higher floors of buildings.

3. Modern ships can _____ bigger storms than old wooden ships.

4. Spaceships carry _____ from Earth to the astronauts at the space station.

C. Choose three words from the box in Part B. Use each word in a sentence.

1. _____
_____

2. _____
_____

3. _____
_____

© Houghton Mifflin Harcourt Publishing Company

Homophones

A. Draw a line under the homophone for each word.

1. see	saw	say	sea
2. row	rue	roe	rose
3. mussels	muscles	missiles	bustles
4. site	sighed	sight	mite
5. morning	morn	mooring	mourning
6. barren	baring	barrow	baron
7. presence	present	presents	absence

B. Complete the paragraph below by filling in each space with the correct word from the box.

rein	mourning	sea	mussel	baron	site	reign	presents
presence	barren	rain	muscle	sight	morning	see	

We got to the beach at seven a.m. Saturday _____. At first, I wished I'd brought an umbrella,

since there was a sprinkle of _____. As we gazed along the shore, it was a lonesome

_____ to _____. Except for us, the expanse of sand was _____ of any life

other than a few strutting seagulls. But soon the weather cleared. The sparkle of the sun on the

waves of the _____ warmed and cheered us. We walked on the beach. My sister discovered

a starfish, and I found a _____ shell. Soon the deserted _____ began to fill up with

the _____ of many people. We joined in a volleyball game and gave our early morning beach

finds as _____ to the winners!

C. Identify two homophone pairs of words in the box. Write a sentence using each word.

1. homophones: _____ and _____

Sentences: _____

_____

2. homophones: _____ and _____

Sentences: _____

_____

© Houghton Mifflin Harcourt Publishing Company

Collaborative Discussion Support

Use this chart to make notes about the plot, setting, and characters of "The Swiss Family Robinson."

Plot
What happened?
_____
_____
_____
_____
_____
_____

Setting
What is the setting? How does the setting affect the plot?
_____
_____
_____
_____
_____
_____

Characters
What are the characters like?
_____
_____
_____
_____
_____

© Houghton Mifflin Harcourt Publishing Company

Compound Words

fishhook	shipwreck	cornfield	half-ripe	gunpowder	sunlight

A. Choose a word from the box to answer each question.

1. What word describes something that would be used to catch a trout?

_____

2. What word describes a substance needed to shoot a musket?

_____

3. What word describes a sight you might see in farm country ?

_____

4. What word means "not yet fully matured"?

_____

5. What word describes a large boat that has sunk?

_____

6. What word describes something lacking on a cloudy day?

_____

B. Complete each sentence with a word from the box.

1. Off the coast of the island, we could still see the _____ of the SS America, which had sunk in 1993.

2. Along with our rods, we brought a variety of _____ for catching different types of fish.

3. In northern Norway, some summer days never get dark, and people have gotten used to twenty-four hours of _____ .

4. Timing is everything with fruit. A _____ apple will not be juicy.

5. In the Revolutionary War, a cannon would not explode unless its _____ was kept dry.

6. A common sight in the heartland of the U.S. is a _____ , since this crop covers about 80 million acres throughout the country.

C. Choose two words from the box. Use each word in a sentence.

1. _____

2. _____

© Houghton Mifflin Harcourt Publishing Company

How English Works

Adverb Clauses

A. Decide whether each underlined adverbial clause is a conditional clause, a clause of comparison/concession, a clause of purpose, or none of the above.

1. <u>Even though the thunderstorm was exciting</u>, we went inside because lightning can be dangerous.

   a. conditional clause   **b.** clause of comparison/concession   **c.** clause of purpose   **d.** none of the above

2. <u>While we were talking</u>, a moose appeared in the distance.

   a. conditional clause   **b.** clause of comparison/concession   **c.** clause of purpose   **d.** none of the above

3. <u>If deer are really hungry</u>, they will eat anything in the garden.

   a. conditional clause   **b.** clause of comparison/concession   **c.** clause of purpose   **d.** none of the above

4. LeRoy moved slowly <u>so that he didn't startle the snake</u>.

   a. conditional clause   **b.** clause of comparison/concession   **c.** clause of purpose   **d.** none of the above

B. Fill in the blanks with a clause that fits the context of the sentence.

1. Ana called out every few seconds so that _____.

2. I heard the wind howl even though _____!

3. I had noticed some tracks while _____.

4. I stay away from porcupines because _____.

5. The National Parks are a great place to go if _____.

C. Choose one topic and write four sentences about it. Use at least one conditional clause, at least one clause of comparison/concession, and at least one clause of purpose. Make sure that you use commas to separate the adverb clauses. You may choose your own topic. Possible topics:

staying home from school sick	giving a presentation	going to the library

1. _____

   _____

2. _____

   _____

3. _____

   _____

4. _____

   _____

© Houghton Mifflin Harcourt Publishing Company

Analyzing the Text

Refer to pp. 25 and 27 of this book to review how you organized information to show cause-and-effect relationships. Use this organizer to think about how the characters change throughout the story. Cite evidence from the text.

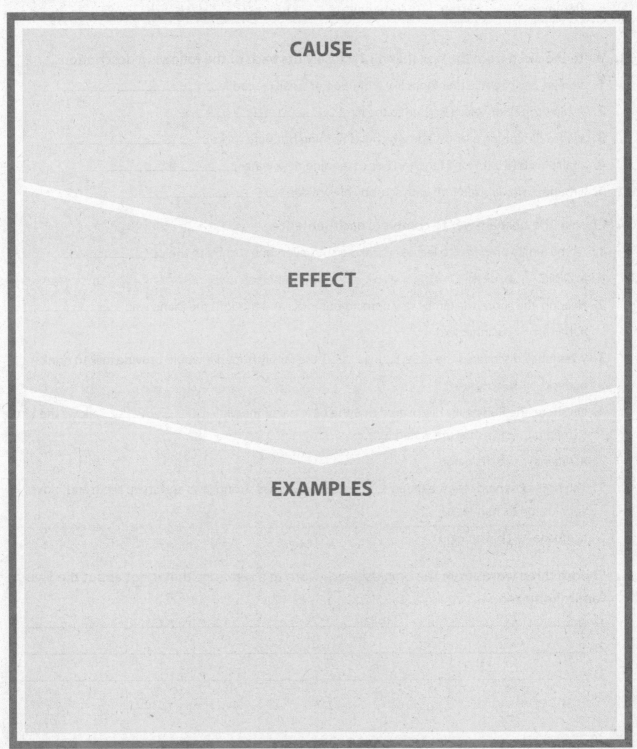

CAUSE

EFFECT

EXAMPLES

© Houghton Mifflin Harcourt Publishing Company

Visual Clues

Use the illustrations in "The Swiss Family Robinson" to help you understand unfamiliar vocabulary, and words that have more than one meaning. Look for context clues.

flamingo	barren	coconut	iguana	deck

A. Write the word from the box that most closely fits each of the following descriptions.

1. a green, scaly reptile that looks like a big frog or small crocodile _____

2. a ship's top floor, which is open to the air _____

3. a word describing a landscape which has nothing but bare rocks _____

4. a tall pink bird with long legs and neck, standing near water _____

5. a round, softball sized fruit with scrubby brown skin _____

B. Choose the best answer to complete each sentence.

1. As the family prepared to leave the sinking ship, everyone rushed to the _____.

    a. cabin   **b.** deck

2. Nearing the shore, the family saw nothing but rocks and thought the island was _____.

    a. barren   **b.** inhabited

3. When they discovered the _____, the family hoped it would provide milk to drink.

    a. deck   **b.** coconut

4. On shore, the Robinsons discovered that the bent bill of the pink _____ allows the bird to feed on small fish in the water.

    a. iguana   **b.** flamingo

5. The boys observed that the green _____ has strong jaws and sharp teeth and moves very fast on its four feet.

    a. iguana   **b.** flamingo

C. Choose three words from the box. Use each word in a sentence that is <u>not</u> about the Swiss Family Robinson.

1. _____

2. _____

3. _____

© Houghton Mifflin Harcourt Publishing Company

Choose a Topic

Use this page with p. 144 of the Student Book to help you choose a topic for Writing a Response to Literature. Your response should include an analysis of how story elements interact and shape a story. How does a main character interact with other characters? Does he or she take bold actions or act carefully? How do different characters respond to challenges in the setting? Comparing and contrasting the challenges faced by characters in two or more stories can be a good way to begin an analysis.

Answer the questions

1. How is the main character in "Torn Away" like the main character in "Swiss Family Robinson"? How are they different?

   These characters are similar because _____.

   These characters are different because _____.

2. How did the setting of "Swiss Family Robinson" influence the characters' actions?

   Three words that describe the setting are _____, _____,

   and _____ .

Write three ideas for your own topic.

Idea 1 _____

_____

_____

_____

Idea 2 _____

_____

_____

_____

Idea 3 _____

_____

_____

_____

_____

© Houghton Mifflin Harcourt Publishing Company

Plan Your Response

Now that you've decided on the main idea for your topic, use this page to support your idea with examples and details. To evaluate your response, use the Response to Literature Rubric available from your online Student Resources or from your teacher.

Characters

The main character is _____.

Other characters are _____.

Describe your impressions of the characters. _____

_____

Describe the relationships between the characters. _____

_____

Explain how the characters change throughout the selection. _____

_____

Plot and Setting

Describe the problem or struggle that the characters face. _____

_____

Characters' Actions

Describe the characters' motivations for their actions. _____

_____

Describe how the characters' actions relate to their feelings or situations. _____

_____

Style Elements

Describe how the author conveys the theme. _____

_____

Explain how the setting is significant to the plot. _____

_____

Cite details that suggest the mode and tone. _____

_____

Make a list of words that emphasize important ideas. _____

_____

© Houghton Mifflin Harcourt Publishing Company

Build Vocabulary

Academic Vocabulary

A. Complete each sentence with the correct word from the box.

specify	specific	specifically

1. Could you _____ what kind of book you'd like to read?

2. My little sister only likes to eat a _____ kind of cereal.

3. I'd like to be able to speak more languages, _____ Japanese.

B. Complete the answers with information from the text.

> A Hawaiian volcano, specifically Kilauea, has entered a state of high activity. We know that this eruption started on a specific date, January 3, 1983, and has continued for decades. Reporters and public officials continuously specify the speed and position of the lava in their reports to the public.

1. Specifically which volcano is in a state of high activity?

It is a Hawaiian volcano, _____.

2. Did the eruption start on a specific date?

We know that _____.

3. What do reporters and officials continuously specify for people?

Reporters and public officials _____.

C. Write a paragraph that restates the facts of the text in Part B. Use all of the words in the box. You may also compare the facts in the passage to another volcanic eruption. Look up another volcano online to compare and contrast volcanic events.

_____

_____

_____

_____

_____

_____

_____

_____

_____

© Houghton Mifflin Harcourt Publishing Company

Finalize Your Plan

WRITING TOOLBOX

Elements of a Response to Literature

Introduction	Decide what you want to say about your topic. Include the characters you will examine.
Main Ideas and Details	State the main points. Include examples that reinforce the points.
Conclusion	Restate the main idea. Use the details that support your analysis.

A. Review the elements of a response to literature above. Describe the elements that you will include in your response.

Introduction _____

_____

_____

Main Ideas and Details _____

_____

_____

Conclusion _____

_____

_____

B. Write a brief summary of your response.

_____

_____

_____

_____

_____

_____

© Houghton Mifflin Harcourt Publishing Company

Vocabulary Review

Here are some of the words you learned in this unit. Choose words from this list and sort them into the categories below. There are many possible correct answers! Also, many of the words fit into more than one category.

asthenosphere	geology	perish	storage
barren	iguana	plate tectonics	survive
clicking	meteorology	plentiful	tectonic
coconut	minute	regular	thud
creak	morning	rumbling	tinkle
dawn	mourning	scarce	unnecessary
erratic	organism	screech	vast
flamingo	Pangaea	specific	vital
fossils	participant	specifically	withstand
geological	participate	specify	work out

Antonym Pairs

1. _____
   _____

2. _____
   _____

Specialized Vocabulary about Earth Sciences

1. _____
2. _____
3. _____
4. _____
5. _____

Onomatopoeia

1. _____
2. _____
3. _____
4. _____
5. _____

Verbs

1. _____
2. _____
3. _____
4. _____
5. _____

© Houghton Mifflin Harcourt Publishing Company

Easily Confused Words

A. Circle the correct word in each sentence. Use the context clues to help you decide.

1. Rachel couldn't decide [whether, weather] she wanted to go on the trip.

2. [It's, Its] too late to sign up for the raffle.

3. Sorry, that's [your, you're] problem.

4. He fixed the [whole, hole] in his coat.

B. Fill in the blanks with the correct word that fits the context of the sentence.

1. I think _____ being a little unfair.

2. The cat scratched behind _____ ear.

3. Roberto didn't answer the _____ question, only part of it.

4. The _____ is terrible today.

5. Carly doesn't think _____ a good idea.

C. Write four sentences, one using *whether* or *weather*, one using *whole* or *hole*, one using *its* or *it's*, and one using *your* or *you're*. Your sentences should demonstrate your understanding of the meaning of each word.

1. _____

_____

_____

2. _____

_____

_____

3. _____

_____

_____

4. _____

_____

_____

© Houghton Mifflin Harcourt Publishing Company

Risk and Exploration

Use words or images to create visual notes that you can add to as you work through this unit.

> *Far better it is to dare mighty things, to win glorious triumphs,*
>
> *even though checkered by failure, than to take rank with those poor*
>
> *spirits who neither enjoy much nor suffer much, because they live in*
>
> *the gray twilight that knows neither victory nor defeat.*
>
> —Theodore Roosevelt, politician

What comes to your mind when you think of risk and exploration? Write or make visual notes.

What are some places that you would like to explore—or places that someone should explore?

_____

_____

What, if anything, is risky about exploring these places?

_____

_____

Is exploring new places always worth the risk? Why or why not?

_____

_____

Why are some people more willing to take these risks than others?

_____

_____

Other notes about risk and exploration

_____

_____

© Houghton Mifflin Harcourt Publishing Company

Academic Vocabulary

As you work through Unit 4, look and listen for these words. Use them when you talk in class and in your writing. Write about your experiences using these words in the last column of the chart.

Word	Definition	Related Forms	My Experiences
complex	• having many connected parts • hard to understand	complexity, complicate, complicated	
potential	• possible • possibility • ability to improve and grow	potent, potentially	
rely	to depend on or trust	reliable, reliability, reliance, self-reliant	
stress	• to emphasize • emphasis • mental or physical pressure	stressed, unstressed, stressed-out, stressful	
valid	based on truth, fact or logic	invalid, validate, validation	

© Houghton Mifflin Harcourt Publishing Company

Antonyms

Think of an antonym for each word below. Remember that a word can have more than one antonym. Write a sentence that uses both the word listed and its antonym.

1. Hope

Antonym: _____

_____

_____

_____

2. False

Antonym: _____

_____

_____

_____

3. Divide

Antonym: _____

_____

_____

_____

4. Temporary

Antonym: _____

_____

_____

_____

5. Destroy

Antonym: _____

_____

_____

_____

© Houghton Mifflin Harcourt Publishing Company

Opposite Day Stories

Follow the directions for the Performance Task on p. 151 of the Student Book to complete this page. Use extra paper, index cards, or a device if you run out of space.

Plan

Work with your group to choose a situation or event. Then think of possible antonyms you could include. For example, the main character in one story might be brave, but in the second story the same character is cowardly.

Our situation is _____.

We'll use these antonym pairs: _____

_____

_____

_____

_____

_____

_____.

Write

Use your plan to write your stories. You will write one story and then use your antonyms to write the second version.

1. Start with something that will get your listeners' attention. What will make them want to hear this story?

_____

_____

2. Put the events in an order that will be easy for listeners to understand.

_____

_____

3. End by telling what the main character learned or what might happen next.

_____

_____

4. Now write the opposite version of this story, using antonyms:

_____

_____

© Houghton Mifflin Harcourt Publishing Company

Collaborative Discussion Support

Look through "StarGazerGuy." Find information to answer the questions below.

How can you tell that StarGazerGuy is glad he visited the planetarium?

_____

_____

_____

_____

Why does he often write in short sentences, like "I don't want to miss that!"

_____

_____

_____

What are some words and phrases that show his excitement?

_____

_____

_____

Does StarGazerGuy think that other young people should visit a planetarium? How can you tell?

_____

_____

_____

_____

Use the above information for the Collaborative Discussion on **Student Book** page 154.

© Houghton Mifflin Harcourt Publishing Company

Critical Vocabulary

A. **Read the sentences below. Circle the definition of each underlined word. Remember that you can look up any unfamiliar words in the dictionary.**

1. The stars on the ceiling were a projected <u>simulation</u> of actual stars. A *simulation* is a

   a. painting.　　**b.** photograph.　　**c.** imitation.

2. The deep, <u>rumbly</u> voice explained how stars are born. *Rumbly* means

   a. unexpected.　　**b.** resonant.　　**c.** educated.

3. I had no idea how <u>complex</u> our solar system is! *Complex* means

   a. complicated.　　**b.** unknown.　　**c.** large.

4. We learned about the different <u>phases</u> of the moon. *Phases* are

   a. stages.　　**b.** different atmospheres.　　**c.** space expeditions.

B. **Choose a word from the box to complete each sentence.**

projected	simulation	complex	astronomers
rumbly	classify	constellations	phases

1. _____ study the moon and the stars.

2. You can easily recognize _____ in the sky on a starry night.

3. After going to the planetarium, I can _____ all the planets in the solar system.

4. Planets were _____ on the ceiling at the planetarium.

5. There are eight different _____ of the moon.

C. **Choose three words from the box in Part B. Use each word in a sentence.**

1. _____

   _____

2. _____

   _____

3. _____

   _____

© Houghton Mifflin Harcourt Publishing Company

Write On! Support

Use this web to brainstorm ideas to include in your blog about looking through a telescope. Go online to find out what you might expect to see through a rooftop planetarium telescope. Put your main idea in the center circle. Then think of three or four points you want to make in your blog. Write them in the smaller circles. Write words or phrases you might include on the lines coming off the smaller circles. Add more circles or lines wherever you need them.

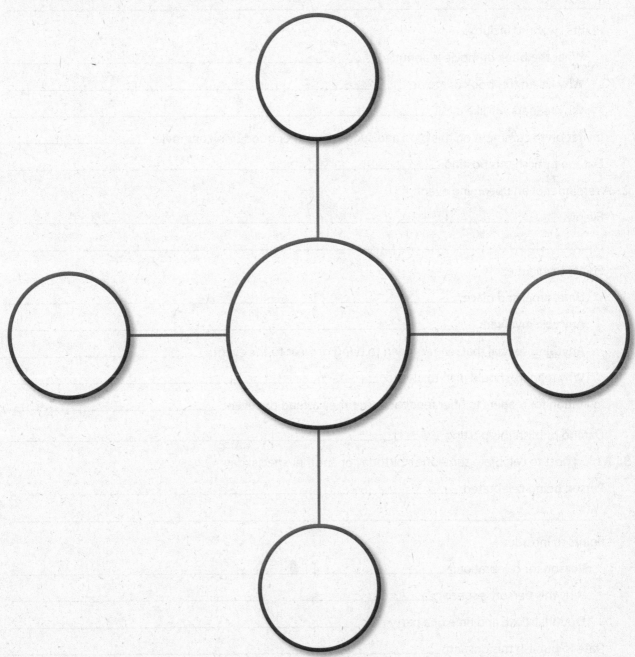

Use to support Write On! on **Student Book** page 154.

© Houghton Mifflin Harcourt Publishing Company

Plan and Write Blog Posts

To evaluate your blog, use the Blog Rubric available from your online Student Resources or from your teacher. Use this page to help plan your three blogs.

1. An entry about a favorite book or movie

My topic: _____

_____

Points I want to include:

What the book or movie is about: _____

Why I liked this book or movie: _____

Why readers will like it: _____

Invitation to comment on this blog and suggest another good book or movie: _____

Date to publish this posting: _____

2. A reminder of an upcoming event

Event: _____

_____

Points to include:

Date, time, and place: _____

Any cost involved: _____

Anything special that readers need to bring or wear to the event: _____

Why readers should plan to attend: _____

Invitation for readers to offer feedback after they attend the event: _____

Date to publish this posting: _____

3. A blog post to celebrate someone's birthday or another special day

Person being celebrated: _____

_____

Points to include:

Reason for celebration: _____

Why this person is special: _____

Optional: Date and time of a party: _____

Date to publish this posting: _____

Use for the Performance Task on **Student Book** pages 154–155.

© Houghton Mifflin Harcourt Publishing Company

Build Vocabulary

Etymology

simulation	constellation	astronomer	telescope	expect

A. Choose the correct answer from the words in the box.

1. What word is formed from a Latin word that means "like" or "similar"? _____

2. What word is formed from a Latin word that means "to await"? _____

3. What word comes from a Greek word that means "far seeing"? _____

4. What word includes a Greek root that means "star"? _____

B. Answer the questions with the correct word.

1. Write a word that belongs to the same word family as *expect*. _____

2. Write a word that belongs to the same word family as *astronomer*. _____

3. Write a word that belongs to the same word family as *simulation*. _____

4. Write a word that belongs to the same word family as *telescope*. _____

C. Look up the etymology of these words in the dictionary: *asthma, barbarian, calculate,* and *chaos*. Write each word and its origin on the lines below. Next, write an additional word that belongs to the same word family. For example, *solar* means "of, relating to, or determined by the sun." The origin of *solar* is the Latin *solarium*. Another term in the same word family is *solar system*.

1. _____

_____

2. _____

_____

3. _____

_____

4. _____

_____

© Houghton Mifflin Harcourt Publishing Company

USE WITH LESSON 4.3   **159**

Compound Sentences

A. Decide if the coordinating conjunction in each sentence should stay as it is, or be changed to another conjunction. Circle the correct answer.

1. Half the travelers headed north, and half went south.

   a. so   **b.** or   **c.** yet   **d.** and

2. I want to take horseback riding lessons, or my parents think it's too dangerous.

   a. but   **b.** and   **c.** so   **d.** or

3. Would you rather explore a city by car, but would you rather see it on foot?

   a. or   **b.** and   **c.** for   **d.** but

4. Today's explorers have GPS, yet we can locate them if necessary.

   a. and   **b.** so   **c.** but   **d.** yet

B. Complete each sentence with a coordinating conjunction.

1. Peggy is a good artist, _____ she could sketch the things we find.

2. I can help you after school tomorrow, _____ I can see you before class starts on Friday.

3. Shackleton was the leader of three expeditions to Antarctica, _____ he also participated in a fourth.

4. People are afraid of change, _____ this fear often holds them back.

5. Adina had traveled on huge planes, _____ she had never been on a ship.

C. Choose one topic and write four sentences about it. Include compound sentences joined by *and*, *but*, *so*, and *or* in your sentences. Possible topics:

talk about some good advice someone has given you	describe your ideal birthday	talk about whether you'd rather be cold or warm

1. _____

   _____

2. _____

   _____

3. _____

   _____

4. _____

   _____

© Houghton Mifflin Harcourt Publishing Company

Information

Answer the questions about *The Intrepid*.

1. Where is the video set? _____

_____

2. What is the Intrepid? _____

_____

3. What were the uses of the Intrepid? _____

_____

4. What is the Enterprise? _____

_____

5. How is the space shuttle different from an airplane? _____

_____

6. How many planes could the Intrepid hold? _____

_____

7. When did the Intrepid become a museum? _____

_____

_____

Compare and Contrast

Think about the video you have just seen. Compare and contrast it with "StarGazerGuy."

1. What common theme do the video and the blog share? _____

_____

_____

_____

2. How are the video and the blog different? _____

_____

_____

_____

3. Would you be more interested in visiting the Intrepid or going to a planetarium? Why? _____

_____

_____

_____

© Houghton Mifflin Harcourt Publishing Company

Critical Vocabulary

A. Circle four words in the Word Bank that you want to know more about. They are all words from the video *Risk and Exploration*.

Word Bank

docked	propellers	recovery vessel	splash-down	enthusiastic	advantages	retrieve
steel	jet engines	capsules	pavilion	competition	flight deck	

B. Watch the video again and listen for the words. Complete the activity.

1. Word: _____

What I think it means: _____

What it means: _____

2. Word: _____

What I think it means: _____

What it means: _____

3. Word: _____

What I think it means: _____

What it means: _____

4. Word: _____

What I think it means: _____

What it means: _____

C. Choose three words that you wrote in Part B. Write a sentence using each word.

1. _____

_____

_____

2. _____

_____

_____

3. _____

_____

_____

© Houghton Mifflin Harcourt Publishing Company

Build Vocabulary

Academic Vocabulary

A. Complete each sentence with the correct word from the box.

complex	complicate

1. You lost the map? That will _____ our efforts to find the beach.

complexity	complex

2. The _____ of these problems makes them really challenging.

complicated	complex

3. The video game focused on time travel, but it didn't explain the story well so it turned out to be too _____ to enjoy.

complicate	complicated

4. The plot of this novel is so _____ that I started taking notes.

B. Complete each sentence.

1. An example of a complicated movie is _____ because _____.

2. I like complex games because _____.

C. Write a paragraph comparing something simple to something complicated using at least two of the words in the box.

complex	complexity	complicate	complicated

_____
_____
_____
_____
_____
_____
_____

© Houghton Mifflin Harcourt Publishing Company

Critical Vocabulary

A. Read the sentences below. Circle the definition of each underlined word. Remember that you can look up any unfamiliar words in the dictionary.

1. I couldn't decide between ecstatic glee and eyeball-clawing horror. *Ecstatic* means

   a. very sick.   **b.** very happy.   **c.** very suspenseful.

2. I didn't want to go to space in a possibly faulty space elevator. *Faulty* means

   a. not working properly.   **b.** very cramped.   **c.** slow.

3. Now climbing a string into space was the most ludicrous thing I could imagine. *Ludicrous* means

   a. funny.   **b.** ridiculous.   **c.** clever.

4. The vast expanse of space surrounded us. An *expanse* is a

   a. dark area.   **b.** wide area.   **c.** confined area.

B. Choose a word from the box to complete each sentence.

ecstatic	glee	faulty	havoc
ascent	expanse	ludicrous	whoop

1. She let out an enormous _____ as they lifted off into space.

2. Zero gravity can really wreak _____ on your body.

3. I love space so much that the thought of becoming an astronaut fills me with _____.

4. The _____ into space from earth can be very rocky.

5. Before its trip to space, the mechanics checked that nothing was _____ with the space shuttle's wiring.

C. Choose three words from the box in Part B. Use each word in a sentence.

1. _____
   _____

2. _____
   _____

3. _____
   _____

© Houghton Mifflin Harcourt Publishing Company

Collaborative Discussion Support

Complete this chart to prepare for a discussion about "Dangerous" on **Student Book** pages 157–159.

Which words, phrases, and details in this excerpt create pictures in your mind?	Cite line numbers where the text evidence can be found.	What do you visualize when you read this word, phrase, or detail?
_____ _____ _____ _____	_____ _____ _____ _____	_____ _____ _____ _____
_____ _____ _____ _____	_____ _____ _____ _____	_____ _____ _____ _____
_____ _____ _____ _____	_____ _____ _____ _____	_____ _____ _____ _____
_____ _____ _____ _____	_____ _____ _____ _____	_____ _____ _____ _____
_____ _____ _____ _____	_____ _____ _____ _____	_____ _____ _____ _____

Use with the Collaborative Discussion on **Student Book** page 160.

© Houghton Mifflin Harcourt Publishing Company

Build Vocabulary

Suffixes

prayers	foxes	battled	running	seconds

A. Choose the correct answer. Circle your answer.

1. How does the suffix in *prayers* change the meaning of the word?

   a. It changes the tense of the verb.   **b.** It changes the number of the noun.

2. How does the suffix in *battled* change the meaning of the word?

   a. It changes the tense of the verb.   **b.** It changes the number of the noun.

3. How does the suffix in *seconds* change the meaning of the word?

   a. It changes the tense of the verb.   **b.** It changes the number of the noun.

4. How does the suffix in *foxes* change the meaning of the word?

   a. It changes the tense of the verb.   **b.** It changes the number of the noun.

5. How does the suffix in *running* change the meaning of the word?

   a. It changes the tense of the verb.   **b.** It changes the number of the noun.

B. Answer each question with the correct noun or verb.

1. Change the number of the noun box. _____

2. Change the tense of the verb look. _____

3. Change the number of the noun bat. _____

4. Change the tense of the verb arrive. _____

5. Change the number of the noun wish. _____

C. Change the tense of each verb shown in the box. Write a sentence, using each verb with its tense changed.

expect	earn	fix	repair

1. _____

2. _____

3. _____

4. _____

© Houghton Mifflin Harcourt Publishing Company

Build Vocabulary

Suffix -ist

A. Complete the table by identifying the root and the suffix for each word.
Write your answers in the blank spaces.

Word	Root	Suffix
archaeologist		
guitarist		
motorist		
cartoonist		
scientist		
artist		

B. Complete each sentence with a word from the table in Part A.

1. Someone who plays the guitar is a(n) _____.

2. A person who operates a motor vehicle is a(n) _____.

3. A(n) _____ is a person who studies archaeology.

4. A(n) _____ is someone who studies science.

5. Someone who creates cartoons is a(n) _____.

6. A person who makes art is a(n) _____.

C. Choose three words from the table in Part A. Use each word in a sentence.
Underline the suffix -ist in each word.

1. _____

_____

2. _____

_____

3. _____

_____

Collaborative Discussion Support

**Look through "Putting Robots to Work." Find information to complete the table.
Make notes below.**

What kinds of information are in "Putting Robots to Work"?

_____

_____

_____

_____

Where might this information have come from?

_____

_____

_____

_____

What makes Mike Wargo, David Lavery, and John Grotzinger qualified to offer information about NASA's space program?

_____

_____

_____

_____

How do you know that the author of "Putting Robots to Work" is qualified to write on this topic?

_____

_____

_____

_____

Use the information for the Collaborative Discussion and Judging the Sources sections on **Student Book** page 168.

© Houghton Mifflin Harcourt Publishing Company

Performance Task

Performance Task Support: Judging Sources

1. Is it evident that Ms. Buckley's sources are trustworthy? How do you know?

_____
_____
_____
_____
_____
_____
_____

2. Give examples of sources that would not be reliable for information about NASA's robot projects.

_____
_____
_____
_____
_____
_____
_____

3. Find at least one more reliable source that talks about a NASA project. How will you know if this source is trustworthy?

_____
_____
_____
_____
_____
_____
_____

© Houghton Mifflin Harcourt Publishing Company

USE WITH STUDENT BOOK p. 169   USE WITH LESSON 11.2   **169**

Academic Vocabulary

A. Complete each sentence with the correct word from the box.

potential	potent

1. The first time I talked to Louise, I had a feeling that she could be a _____ friend.

potent	potentially

2. Farhad thinks cameras are a _____ tool for storytelling.

potentially	potential

3. We planted our avocado seed, so if it grows well, we could _____ be selling avocados in ten years.

potent	potential

4. Scott has real _____ to become an Olympic athlete.

B. Read the passage and answer the questions.

> Jeff was one of the first people to see the amazing potential of tablet computers. He believed that a hundred million people would potentially read books on tablets in the future. As tablets continue to become more potent, more people will find more interesting ways to use them.

1. What was Jeff one of the first people to see?

   He was one of the first people to see _____

2. How many people might read books on tablets in the future? _____

   _____ might read books on tablets in the future.

3. What do tablet computers continue to do?

   Tablet computers _____.

C. Using a word from the box, write a sentence about something you feel you have the potential to do.

potential	potentially

_____

_____

© Houghton Mifflin Harcourt Publishing Company

Create a Timeline

As you listen to the podcast, write each important event in sequential order.
Place one event in each box.

© Houghton Mifflin Harcourt Publishing Company

Critical Vocabulary

A. Read the sentences below. Circle the definition of each underlined word. Remember that you can look up any unfamiliar words in the dictionary.

1. The <u>ascent</u> was the most difficult part of our journey across the mountain. An *ascent* is

   a. an upward climb.   **b.** a hole.   **c.** a long distance.

2. I was so dehydrated that the tea tasted like the best thing I ever had in my life. *Dehydrated* means

   a. having a cold.   **b.** needing water.   **c.** wanting food.

3. Iñaki would <u>disapprove</u> of climbing Mt. Everest with oxygen. *Disapprove* means

   a. have an unfavorable opinion.   **b.** have jealous feelings.   **c.** be impressed.

4. You must have perfect balance while climbing a <u>steep</u> ridge. *Steep* means

   a. sharply angled.   **b.** snowy.   **c.** frightening.

B. Choose a word from the box to complete each sentence.

dehydrated	summit	ascent	disapprove
steep	vertical	claustrophobic	

1. It is not unusual to feel _____ in small spaces.

2. He looked down in fear at the _____ ice and rock face.

3. Joby Ogwyn wanted to make the fastest _____ of Mount Everest.

4. Many mountaineers cannot make it to a mountain's _____ without oxygen and supplies.

5. The tall rock face almost appeared _____ to the overwhelmed mountain climber.

C. Choose three words from the box in Part B. Use each word in a sentence.

1. _____

   _____

2. _____

   _____

3. _____

   _____

© Houghton Mifflin Harcourt Publishing Company

Retell the Story

Discuss Joby's adventure on Mount Everest with your group. Use this page to focus on his language and the sequence of his story. You will be retelling the story in your own words.

1. What do you notice about the kind of language that Joby uses in his podcast? Is it formal, casual, amusing, or dramatic? _____

_____

2. Use the graphic organizer to retell the main events in Joby's story. Describe events as they occurred (beginning, middle, and end).

```
┌─────────────────────────────────────────┐
│ Beginning _____ │
│ _____ │
│ _____ │
│ _____ │
│ _____ │
└─────────────────────────────────────────┘
                    │
                    ▼
┌─────────────────────────────────────────┐
│ Middle _____ │
│ _____ │
│ _____ │
│ _____ │
│ _____ │
└─────────────────────────────────────────┘
                    │
                    ▼
┌─────────────────────────────────────────┐
│ End _____ │
│ _____ │
│ _____ │
│ _____ │
│ _____ │
└─────────────────────────────────────────┘
```

© Houghton Mifflin Harcourt Publishing Company

Build Vocabulary

Expressions

A. Circle the correct answer.

1. What slang expression means "to relax"?

   a. chill out   **b.** no pressure

2. What slang expression means "amazing"?

   a. super fit   **b.** cool

3. What slang expression means "in great physical shape"?

   a. super fit   **b.** cool

4. What slang expression means "the state of being under a great deal of pressure"?

   a. no pressure   **b.** chill out

5. What slang expression means "doing what you want to do without worrying about what others think"?

   a. doing your thing   **b.** every man for himself

B. Complete each sentence with a phrase from the box.

chill out	doing your thing	every man for himself	cool	no pressure	super fit

1. Oh, Enrico, _____ and stop worrying. You'll do fine on the test.

2. Hey, _____, they only want you to have your entire role in the play memorized by tomorrow.

3. Because Mark lifts weights every day he is _____.

4. You are _____ if you are doing what you want to do no matter what people think.

5. In this company no one helps anyone else with anything. It's _____.

C. Choose four slang expressions from the box. Use each slang expression in a sentence.

1. _____

   _____

2. _____

   _____

3. _____

   _____

4. _____

   _____

© Houghton Mifflin Harcourt Publishing Company

Critical Vocabulary

A. Read the sentences below. Circle the definition of each underlined word. Remember that you can look up any unfamiliar words in the dictionary.

1. A fleet of ships left the Chinese <u>port</u> of Nanjing. A *port* is a

   a. harbor where ships are stationed.   **b.** magnificent city.   **c.** capital city.

2. Zheng He had an <u>imposing</u> manner. *Imposing* means

   a. impressive.   **b.** cruel.   **c.** busy.

3. The <u>fleet</u> sailed south from the China Sea to Indonesia and across to India. A *fleet* is a

   a. group of officials.   **b.** collection of ships.   **c.** traders.

4. Zhu Di wanted to show off his power and make <u>alliances</u> with other kingdoms. *Alliances* are

   a. arguments.   **b.** longstanding wars.   **c.** beneficial relationships.

B. Choose a word from the box to complete each sentence.

port	ambassador	operation	grandeur
imposing	alliances	fleet	expert

1. The _____ of the fleets impressed many people at the time.

2. Successfully crossing the ocean must have been a very difficult _____ in that time.

3. _____ agree that Zheng He created the greatest fleet in the world.

4. Zheng He became China's _____ to other countries during his many travels.

5. The _____ of ships carried many goods to trade with during its travels.

C. Choose three words from the box in Part B. Use each word in a sentence.

1. _____

   _____

2. _____

   _____

3. _____

   _____

© Houghton Mifflin Harcourt Publishing Company

Evaluate Arguments

A. Determine which underlined word is the coordinating conjunction in each sentence.

1. Some books tell only what's good about someone, and these are usually less interesting than more complex and honest biographies.

   a. Some books   **b.** someone, and these   **c.** complex and honest   **d.** less interesting than more

2. Very early explorers are difficult to research, but the author explains how important they are.

   a. difficult to research   **b.** explains how important   **c.** research, but the author   **d.** Very early explorers

3. Scientific failures are always valuable, and the author points out what they can teach us.

   a. failures are always   **b.** valuable, and the author   **c.** are always valuable   **d.** points out what they

4. The author favors medical treatment by robots, and argues that they could already be treating contagious diseases under a doctor's guidance.

   a. robots, and argues   **b.** treatment by robots   **c.** they could already be   **d.** diseases under a doctor's

B. Fill in the blanks with an independent clause that fits the context of the sentence.

1. Robots already perform medical operations, and _____

   _____ .

2. The article on Amelia Earhart claims to know exactly what happened to this aviation pioneer, but

   _____ .

3. Each chapter focuses on one decade of the 20th century, and _____

   _____ .

4. The two authors disagree about the use of robots in our personal lives, but

   _____ .

5. The author compares the two voyages, and _____

   _____ .

C. Choose one topic and write at least two sentences about it. Include compound sentences joined by *and* and *but* in your sentences. Possible topics:

talk about a hobby you enjoy	talk about something you do to relax	describe your greatest strength

1. _____

   _____

2. _____

   _____

© Houghton Mifflin Harcourt Publishing Company

Build Vocabulary

Context Clues

port	commanding	ambassador	complex	alliances	innovation

A. Choose the correct word from the box to answer each question.

1. Which word describes a person with a powerful presence that people respect? _____

2. Which word means "a person who represents his or her country in another country"? _____

3. Which word means "unions between people, groups, or countries"? _____

4. Which word means "the act or process of introducing new ideas"? _____

5. Which word means "complicated"? _____

B. Complete each sentence with the correct word from the box.

1. The United States has military and trade _____ with many countries.

2. As the _____ to France, Mr. Morel represents the interests and concerns of the United States.

3. His _____ presence combined with his vast knowledge of football made all the players respect him.

4. It was a complicated and _____ math problem, and Ellen had a difficult time solving it.

5. The ship pulled into _____ so that it could unload its cargo.

C. Choose five words from the box. Use each word in a sentence.

1. _____

_____

2. _____

_____

3. _____

_____

4. _____

_____

5. _____

_____

© Houghton Mifflin Harcourt Publishing Company

Collaborative Discussion Support

Look through "Admiral of the Western Seas" on pp 173–175 of the Student Book.
Find information to complete the organizer below.

1. What are some questions that this author might have asked first, before he knew much about Zheng He?

_____
_____
_____
_____

2. After the author gathered information to answer those questions, what are some other questions he might have asked? (These questions might not have been answered in the final draft of the article.)

_____
_____
_____
_____
_____
_____

3. What else are you curious about, related to this topic? What would you like to know about this admiral or his expeditions?

_____
_____
_____
_____
_____

Use the information for the Collaborative Discussion on **Student Book** page 176.

© Houghton Mifflin Harcourt Publishing Company

Academic Vocabulary

A. Complete each sentence with the correct word from the box.

rely	reliance

1. The baseball team _____ on their star pitcher to help them win.

self-reliant	reliability

2. People who live in solar-powered houses and grow their own food are _____.

reliance	reliable

3. When I bake, I often make lemon bars because I have a _____ recipe.

reliance	reliability

4. George won't use cloud computing because he questions its _____.

B. Complete each sentence.

1. I can rely on my friend because he/she _____.

2. A dictionary is a reliable source for _____.

C. Write a paragraph about how and why some students rely on computers.

_____

_____

_____

_____

_____

_____

_____

_____

_____

© Houghton Mifflin Harcourt Publishing Company

Visual Clues

| enormous | alliances | grandeur | extent | extraordinary | expeditions |

A. Choose the correct word from the box to answer each question.

1. Which word means "range, distance, or space that is covered"? _____

2. Which word means "very unusual"? _____

3. Which word means "splendor and impressiveness"? _____

4. Which word means "journeys made by groups of people for a specific purpose"? _____

5. Which word means "very large in size"? _____

B. Choose the correct word from the box to complete each sentence.

1. Admiral Zheng He's many _____ sent him to kingdoms around the Indian Ocean.

2. The size of Zheng He's ships were _____, especially when compared to the size of a typical ship.

3. During his travels Zheng He made _____ with many kingdoms in Africa and Asia.

4. The _____ of Zheng He's voyages can be seen on the map that charts the places he traveled to.

5. What Zheng He achieved was not a common feat, it was in fact _____.

C. Choose three words from the box. Use each word in a sentence that is <u>not</u> about Zheng He, his ships, or his travels.

1. _____

   _____

   _____

2. _____

   _____

   _____

3. _____

   _____

   _____

© Houghton Mifflin Harcourt Publishing Company

Multiple-Meaning Words

A. Choose the response that correctly defines the underlined word as it is used in the sentence.

1. We asked the star for her autograph.

   a. well-known and talented performer   **b.** an object in space made of burning gas

2. Jorge spent a long time studying for the test.

   a. period of seconds, minutes, hours, or days

   b. the particular minute or hour shown on a watch or clock

3. His ability to strike out even the best hitters made Manny a legend in our town.

   a. a story from the past that is believed to be true but can't be proven to be true

   b. a famous person known for doing something extremely well

4. Can you give me change for ten dollars?

   a. bills or coins in small denominations   **b.** become different

5. Phil decided to spend the afternoon with his cousin.

   a. to allow time to pass while doing something   **b.** use money to pay for something

B. Define each underlined word as it is used in the sentence.

1. John Henry is an American legend about a steel-driving man.

   _____

2. I am going to take a shower and change my clothes.

   _____

3. The stars are so bright against the night sky!

   _____

4. He was the commander of the Pacific fleet.

   _____

5. I was thrilled to hear that my favorite actress would star in the movie.

   _____

C. Choose one of the underlined words from Part A. Use the word in two sentences that show different meanings of the word.

Sentence 1: _____

Sentence 2: _____

© Houghton Mifflin Harcourt Publishing Company

Critical Vocabulary

A. Read the sentences below. Circle the definition of each underlined word. Remember that you can look up any unfamiliar words in the dictionary.

1. The Corps of Discovery, led by Meriwether Lewis and William Clark, arrived in St. Louis yesterday at noon. A *corps* is a

   a. group.   **b.** game.   **c.** leader.

2. Their primary objective was to look for a water route along the Missouri River from the center of the continent to the Pacific Ocean. An *objective* is a

   a. dream.   **b.** purpose.   **c.** thought.

3. The expedition was outfitted with thousands of pounds of supplies. *Outfitted* means

   a. equipped.   **b.** overwhelmed.   **c.** rich.

4. Other than the location of St. Louis and the locations of the Columbia and Missouri rivers, the map was a distressing blank. *Distressing* means

   a. causing anxiety.   **b.** wrinkly.   **c.** causing excitement.

B. Choose a word from the box to complete each sentence.

corps	objective	interactions	lowlands
route	distressing	leading	outfitted

1. We studied the _____ that Lewis and Clark took throughout the west.

2. The _____ between Lewis and Clark and the Native Americans were mostly friendly.

3. The explorers found good weather in the _____ before crossing the mountains.

4. _____ mapmakers helped the explorers by creating the best maps possible.

5. Expeditions that are _____ with enough supplies should be successful.

C. Choose three words from the box in Part B. Use each word in a sentence.

1. _____

   _____

2. _____

   _____

3. _____

   _____

© Houghton Mifflin Harcourt Publishing Company

Complex Sentences

A. Determine which underlined word is the subordinate conjunction in each sentence.

1. I keep thinking it's later than it is, because the sun sets so early in the winter.

    a. later <u>than</u> it is   **b.** sets <u>so</u> early   **c.** is, <u>because</u> the sun   **d.** <u>in</u> the winter

2. Although Rosa enjoys most kinds of food, she can't eat tomatoes.

    a. <u>Although</u> Rosa enjoys   **b.** <u>can't</u> eat tomatoes   **c.** kinds <u>of</u> food   **d.** food, <u>she</u> can't

3. Don't record your measurements until you've double-checked them.

    a. <u>Don't</u> record your   **b.** double-checked <u>them</u>   **c.** record <u>your</u> measurements
    d. measurements <u>until</u> you've

4. Eugene stayed home from school while he had the flu.

    a. <u>while</u> he had   **b.** home <u>from</u> school   **c.** Eugene stayed <u>home</u>   **d.** he had <u>the</u> flu

B. Fill in the blanks with a dependent clause that fits the context of the sentence.

1. Before _____, Jean found it difficult to stay on task.

2. Jorge realized he needs glasses when _____.

3. Nobody could understand us until _____.

4. Although _____, it doesn't perform as well as other models.

5. I can't help you solve that equation because _____.

C. Choose one topic and write four sentences about it. Include at least three dependent clauses introduced with subordinate conjunctions in your sentences. Possible topics:

your favorite holiday	whether you're a dog person or a cat person	whether you'd rather be inside or outside

1. _____

_____

2. _____

_____

3. _____

_____

4. _____

_____

Collaborative Discussion Support

Think about how you would write a news account of an historical event. Work with your partner using three separate steps to complete the process: write a draft, revise and edit, and publish your work. You are writing for the news, so remember to tell who, what, where, when, why, and how. Add more steps below if you need them.

1. Choose a topic:

_____
_____
_____
_____
_____
_____

2. What would you need to find out? Remember to use the 5 W's and 1 H as a guide.

_____
_____
_____
_____
_____
_____

3. What steps would you have to follow to research information for the article?

_____
_____
_____
_____
_____
_____
_____

Use the information for the Collaborative Discussion on **Student Book** page 183.

© Houghton Mifflin Harcourt Publishing Company

Academic Vocabulary

A. Choose the correct answer from the box.

stressed	stress

1. Nurses who care for very sick patients have to deal with a lot of _____.

unstressed	stressed

2. The second syllable in the word "potential" should be _____.

unstressed	stressful

3. Meter in poetry is a regular pattern of stressed and _____ syllables.

stressed-out	stressful

4. Being an astronaut must be really exciting but also very _____.

B. Read the passage and answer the questions.

Kim is an adventurous shopper. She goes to traditional markets in different countries and looks for gifts for her friends, but sometimes it's a stressful hobby. In Vietnam, she felt particularly stressed-out after a cyclo (pedicab) ride through busy traffic. In a Moroccan souk (market), she kept stressing that the shoes she wanted weren't the right size but she didn't know enough Arabic to explain herself more clearly. However, Kim says she finds the stress of shopping exciting.

1. What is Kim's stressful hobby?

She gets into stressful situations while _____.

2. When did she feel stressed out in Vietnam?

She felt stressed-out _____.

3. What was she stressing in the Moroccan souk?

She was trying to stress _____.

4. Does Kim enjoy shopping?

She says _____.

C. Write a sentence about something that stresses you out.

_____

_____

© Houghton Mifflin Harcourt Publishing Company

Research a Topic

Think of a topic that interests you. It might be an event or issue in the news today, an event in history, a well-known person, the history of your favorite sport, or any other topic that would be acceptable to discuss at school. Then follow the steps in the Performance Task assignment:

1. List your topic and then write all the words and phrases you know about it.

My topic is _____ .

_____

_____

_____

_____

_____

_____

_____

2. Use those words and phrases to narrow your topic. For example, instead of writing about a sports rivalry between two colleges, you might write about a big game that was greatly influenced by this rivalry. Next, circle the words and phrases you listed that relate closely to your narrowed topic.

My more specific topic is _____ .

Using a search engine, type in each circled word and phrase as a search term.

3. Use minus signs, asterisks, and/or quotation marks to locate relevant information in your online search.

Here are search terms I combined with:

A minus sign: _____

An asterisk: _____

Quotation marks: _____

4. The advanced search feature that was most helpful for me was _____

_____ .

It helped by _____

_____ .

Use the information for the Performance Task on **Student Book** page 183.

© Houghton Mifflin Harcourt Publishing Company

Speak Out! Support

You're a reporter.

Lewis and Clark have just come to your town.

What questions would you like to ask the townspeople about their impressions and opinions?

Some Ideas:

- What are your thoughts about Lewis and Clark's expedition?
- What did Lewis and Clark say about the regions they visited?
- How might their journey affect our young nation?
- Will you travel west?

Now write your questions.

1. _____
   _____

2. _____
   _____

3. _____
   _____

How will you answer your questions?

1. _____
   _____
   _____

2. _____
   _____
   _____

3. _____
   _____
   _____

© Houghton Mifflin Harcourt Publishing Company

Expressions

sick as a dog	the ball is in your court	bite off more than you can chew
hit the nail on the head	sit on the fence	the whole nine yards

A. Choose the correct phrase from the box to answer each question.

1. Which idiom means "to try to do something that is too much or too difficult to do"?

   _____

2. Which idiom means "do or say something exactly right"? _____

3. Which idiom means "it's up to you to decide or take the next step"? _____

4. Which idiom means "everything, all of it"? _____

5. Which idiom describes someone who does not want to choose or make

   a decision? _____

B. Complete each sentence with a phrase from the box.

1. Enrico _____ when he said that we should stop arguing among

   ourselves and get to work to solve the problem.

2. As you plan your project make sure that you don't _____.

3. You have to make a choice. Don't _____ .

4. Kim was out of school all week because she was _____ .

5. Marcus is a wonderful team player. He always goes _____ .

C. Choose four idioms from the box. Use each idiom in a sentence.

1. _____

   _____

2. _____

   _____

3. _____

   _____

4. _____

© Houghton Mifflin Harcourt Publishing Company

Specialized Vocabulary

| shore | route | ashore | rivers | lifeboats | raft | docks |

A. Choose the correct word from the box to answer each question.

1. Which word means "a way to get from one place to another"? _____

2. Which word means "land along the edge of a sea, lake, or other large body of water"? _____

3. Which word means "places on the water to load and unload supplies or goods

from a ship or boat"? _____

4. Which word means "a flat structure for support or transportation on water"? _____

5. Which word means "small boats carried on a ship that are used for saving the lives of passengers"?

_____

B. Complete each sentence with the correct word from the box.

1. The _____ flow through the country and eventually empty into the ocean.

2. The cruise ship vacationers went _____ to do some shopping on the island.

3. What _____ will you take to get from our school to the concert hall?

4. Unfortunately, the doomed and sinking *Titanic* did not have enough _____ for all of its

passengers.

5. The inflatable _____ was all the family had to stay afloat after their boat sank.

C. Choose three words from the box. Use each word in a sentence.

1. _____

_____

_____

2. _____

_____

_____

3. _____

_____

_____

© Houghton Mifflin Harcourt Publishing Company

Visual Clues for Idioms

A. Choose the response that correctly defines the underlined idiom as it is used in each sentence.

1. The idiom "from every walk of life" means _____ .
   a. from every status and occupation   b. from groups of people who enjoy walking

2. How might a "mother hen" treat her grown children?
   a. She would encourage them to be independent.   b. She would fuss over them.

3. If a sailor sails into the "great unknown," where is he or she going?
   a. someplace far away   b. vast, unexplored territories

4. If an athlete has a challenging workout "under her belt," what has happened?
   a. He or she successfully completed the workout.   b. He or she decided the workout was too difficult.

5. If you do volunteer work in your "downtime" when do you volunteer?
   a. when you're not busy   b. when you're feeling down or depressed

B. Choose the word from the box that most closely fits each of the following descriptions of an illustration.

from every walk of life	**great unknown**	**under his belt**
mother hen	**downtime**	**rough going**

1. ship sailing into the sunrise with no visible landmarks around _____

2. man playing a guitar, other men singing; in the background men clowning around _____

3. Shackleton personally shaving one of his men to encourage all of his men to keep up with personal hygiene _____

4. men representing different occupations such as baseball player, bussinessman, and laborer _____

5. tired-looking men lifting heavy bags of supplies; in the background men laboring to haul the ship over and through pack ice _____

C. Choose three words or phrases from the box in B. Use each word in a sentence that is <u>not</u> about Shackleton or the hardships endured by the men on the *Endurance*.

1. _____
   _____

2. _____
   _____

3. _____
   _____

© Houghton Mifflin Harcourt Publishing Company

Connect Ideas

A. **Determine which word from each sentence is the noun form of a verb.**

1. Your comparison between my work and my friend's work makes me uncomfortable.

   a. between   **b.** uncomfortable   **c.** comparison   **d.** and

2. Kara's suggestion that we go to the store seemed like a good idea to him.

   a. seemed   **b.** suggestion   **c.** Kara's   **d.** to

3. NASA's discovery of potential signs of life on Mars really excites Siobhan.

   a. discovery   **b.** excites   **c.** potential   **d.** on

4. Our discussion of all the options exhausted me.

   a. exhausted   **b.** all   **c.** Our   **d.** discussion

B. **Complete each sentence with a noun form of a verb.**

1. Your _____ on linguistics made it seem more interesting to me.

2. My sister's _____ from cancer has been an enormous relief.

3. My family's _____ of the options helped us figure out what we wanted.

4. Chantal's _____ that we go dancing turned out to be a great idea.

5. This author's _____ of the data suggests that funding education helps the economy.

C. **Choose one topic and write four sentences about it. Include at least two noun forms of verbs to join ideas together in your sentences. Possible topics:**

talk about something you're looking forward to	talk about something you miss	talk about a big change in your life

1. _____

   _____

2. _____

   _____

3. _____

   _____

4. _____

   _____

© Houghton Mifflin Harcourt Publishing Company

Collaborative Discussion Support

Look through "Ernest Shackleton." Find information to answer the questions below.

Which panels in this story help bring the setting to life? Describe what you like about the ones you chose.

_____
_____
_____
_____
_____

Do the words and pictures always match? If not, in which panels?

_____
_____
_____
_____
_____

Which illustrations tell more of the story than the text on that panel?

_____
_____
_____
_____
_____

Use the information for the Collaborative Discussion on **Student Book** page 192
and in "Ernest Shackleton."

© Houghton Mifflin Harcourt Publishing Company

Analyzing the Text Support

Complete this chart to analyze "Ernest Shackleton", Student Book pages 185–191.

Use the information for Analyzing the Text on **Student Book** page 192.

Analyze	
How does the author build suspense, or the growing feeling of tension and excitement, in the story?	Cite text evidence.

Infer	
Reread page 190. How would you describe what the characters are feeling?	Cite text evidence.

© Houghton Mifflin Harcourt Publishing Company

Build Vocabulary

Homophones

A. Circle the correct homophone to complete each sentence.

1. _____ cold outside today.

   It's   Its

2. The cat licked _____ paws.

   it's   its

3. Would you like _____ go to the movies with me today?

   to   too

4. Len would like to go to the park with us _____.

   two   too

5. I brought _____ apples, one for you and one for me.

   too   two

B. Complete each sentence with the correct homophone.

there	their	they're

1. Do you see that bird over _____?

2. Josh and Eric said _____ going to come over later.

3. Mia and Olly like to ride _____ bikes in the park.

C. Use each homophone in the box in Part B in a sentence.

1. _____

   _____

2. _____

   _____

3. _____

   _____

© Houghton Mifflin Harcourt Publishing Company

Performance Task

Plan Research Topics

Answer the questions below to help you plan your research report on exploration.

What are some types of exploration you would like to learn more about?

_____

_____

Use the library and/or the Internet to search for information about several of the topics you have listed. What did you find interesting about each topic?

Topic 1 _____

What I found interesting

_____

_____

Topic 2 _____

What I found interesting

_____

_____

Topic 3 _____

What I found interesting

_____

_____

Topic 4 _____

What I found interesting

_____

_____

Choose a Topic

Which topic will you choose to write about?

_____

_____

What part of the topic will you write about?

_____

_____

© Houghton Mifflin Harcourt Publishing Company

Make an Outline

After you have gathered your sources, taken notes, and checked your facts, use the outline below to plan your research report. To evaluate your work, use the Research Report Rubric available from your online Student Resources or from your teacher.

Main Idea

Write the main idea for your research report.

_____

_____

_____

Supporting Details

What details will you use to support your main idea?

A. Supporting detail: _____

_____

B. Supporting detail: _____

_____

C. Supporting detail: _____

_____

What text evidence from the sources can you use?

_____

_____

_____

What primary and secondary sources will you use?

_____

_____

_____

What are some ideas for the title of your research report?

_____

_____

© Houghton Mifflin Harcourt Publishing Company

Academic Vocabulary

A. Read each statement and decide whether the reasoning is *valid* or *invalid*.

1. I brought an umbrella since the sky was filled with dark clouds. _____

2. I brought an umbrella since I heard there might be a snowstorm today. _____

3. Karen wanted to pass her driving exam, so she decided to take lessons. _____

B. Complete the sentences below with information from the text.

Nia went to the principal's office to ask if she could leave to go to the doctor. When Principal Kwon heard her request, he said, "A doctor's appointment is a valid reason for being absent. You just need to ask the doctor's office to validate your visit with a letter. When you come back to school, bring me the validation and everything will be fine."

1. What is a valid reason for being absent?

   A valid reason for being absent is _____.

2. What does Nia need to ask the doctor's office to do?

   She needs to ask them _____.

3. When she returns to school, what must Nia do?

   She must _____.

C. When a student works hard in school, he or she can receive different kinds of validation. Write a paragraph about why validation is important for students.

_____
_____
_____
_____
_____
_____
_____

© Houghton Mifflin Harcourt Publishing Company

Finalize Your Plan

WRITING TOOLBOX

Elements of a Research Project

Introduction	In the introduction, present your main idea. Include an interesting fact, question, or quotation.
Main Idea and Details	You can have one paragraph or more than one. If you have more than one, each paragraph should include a main idea and supporting details.
Conclusion	The conclusion should follow and sum up how the details support your main idea.
Bibliography	A bibliography is a list of sources that you have consulted or cited in your report.

A. Review the elements of a research project above. Describe the elements that you will use in your report.

Introduction _____

_____

Main Idea and Details _____

_____

Conclusion _____

_____

Bibliography _____

_____

_____

B. Write a brief summary of your project.

_____

_____

_____

_____

© Houghton Mifflin Harcourt Publishing Company

Unit Review

Here are some of the words you learned in this unit. Choose words from this list and sort them into the categories below. There are many possible correct answers.

alliances	distressing	objective	stressed
ambassador	enormous	operation	stressed-out
ascent	expert	port	stressful
astronomer	extraordinary	potential	time
change	fleet	reliable	unstressed
claustrophobic	grandeur	simulation	valid
complex	imposing	speed	vertical
constellation	innovation	star	water
disapprove	invalid	stress	

Multiple-Meaning Words

1. Word: _____

   Definition 1: _____

   Definition 2: _____

2. Word: _____

   Definition 1: _____

   Definition 2: _____

Adjectives

1. _____
2. _____
3. _____
4. _____
5. _____

Words with the Root "stress"

1. _____
2. _____
3. _____
4. _____
5. _____

Nouns

1. _____
2. _____
3. _____
4. _____
5. _____

© Houghton Mifflin Harcourt Publishing Company

Easily Confused Words

A. Circle the correct word in each sentence. Use the context clues to help you decide which word is correct.

1. We found the perfect [sight, site, cite] to set up our tent.

2. It's important not to [desert, dessert] your friends.

3. This paper doesn't [sight, site, cite] enough sources.

4. For [desert, dessert] Mikki made some delicious brownies.

| sight | site | cite | desert | dessert |

B. Complete each sentence with the correct word from the box.

1. Plenty of people live in the _____, but it isn't easy.

2. I've _____ several unusual birds in this park.

3. There's a lot of good information about penguins on this _____.

4. This movie theater is pretty much _____ in the middle of the day.

5. That fireworks display was an amazing _____.

C. Write four sentences, two using sight, site, or cite and two using desert (as a noun or a verb) or dessert. Your sentences should demonstrate your understanding of the meaning of each word.

1. _____
   _____
   _____

2. _____
   _____
   _____

3. _____
   _____
   _____

4. _____
   _____
   _____

© Houghton Mifflin Harcourt Publishing Company

The Stuff of Consumer Culture

What is our role in a consumer culture?

What do you think of when you hear the term *consumerism*?
You can make visual notes or write.

What objects do you think of when you think of consumerism?

_____

_____

What activity do you connect with consumerism?

_____

_____

Name two things you buy too much of.

_____

_____

What is one thing people throw away too much?

_____

_____

What is one natural resource people waste?

_____

_____

© Houghton Mifflin Harcourt Publishing Company

Academic Vocabulary

As you work through Unit 5, look and listen for these words. Use them when you talk in class and in your writing. Write about your experiences using these words in the last column of the chart.

Word	Definition	Related Forms	My Experiences
attitude	a way of thinking or feeling about something		
consume	• to buy or use things or services • to eat, drink, or use up	consumer, consumption, consumerism	
goal	• a purpose or aim • the area that players try to get a ball or puck into • points scored in a game	goal-oriented	
purchase	• to buy • the act of buying • something that is bought	purchaser	
technology	• scientific knowledge used to invent useful things or to solve problems • electronic or digital products	technological, technologically	

© Houghton Mifflin Harcourt Publishing Company

Denotation v. Connotation

Remember, *denotation* is a word's primary, literal definition. *Connotation* covers the more emotional, suggestive meaning of a word.

> You want the car you buy to have a **powerful** engine, not just a **large** one.

> You want the television you buy to have a **lifelike** picture, not just a **clear** one.

> You want the technology you buy to be **state-of-the-art**, not just **new**.

> You want the fabric of the sweater you buy to be **luxurious**, not just **soft**.

> You want the house you buy to be **palatial**, not just **big**.

Using the highlighted words from the chart above, finish each sentence with the word that has the right connotation for the context.

1. I want the couch pillows to be _____ but still firm.

2. The picture on my tablet is _____ enough, I guess.

3. The truck will have to have a very _____ engine to tow that trailer.

4. For this complicated new project, I'm going to need _____ software.

Write two sentences like the ones in the boxes above. Each sentence should contain both connotative and denotative words or expressions.

1. _____

_____

2. _____

_____

© Houghton Mifflin Harcourt Publishing Company

Writing a Product Advertisement

Plan

1. What product will you choose to advertise? _____

2. What do you like about this product? _____

3. What words could you choose to describe it?

neutral words

_____

_____

positive words

_____

_____

Write

1. Catch the reader's attention! What is your first line?

_____

_____

_____

_____

2. What do you want to say about the product?

_____

_____

_____

_____

3. Wrap it up!

_____

_____

_____

_____

© Houghton Mifflin Harcourt Publishing Company

Collaborative Discussion Support

Discussing the Purpose

1. What are some of the sequence signal words in the blog "Fashionisto"?

_____

_____

2. How do these words help the reader understand the steps of making the t-shirt?

_____

_____

Exploring the Topic

1. What is something you have made or would like to make from something else?

_____

_____

2. How would you do it?

_____

_____

Staying Safe

1. What happens to photos you post to the Internet and who gets to see them?

_____

_____

2. Can you keep strangers from copying your photos and using them however they want?

_____

_____

3. What kinds of photos should you be careful about posting?

_____

_____

© Houghton Mifflin Harcourt Publishing Company

Critical Vocabulary

A. Read the sentences below. Circle the definition of each underlined word. Remember that you can look up any unfamiliar words in the dictionary.

1. Time to be a creator rather than a <u>consumer</u>! A *consumer* is

   a. an artist. **b.** a person who buys products. **c.** an economist.

2. Be sure to work in a well-<u>ventilated</u> area when working with bleach. *Ventilated* means

   a. well-lit **b.** heated. **c.** airy.

3. The <u>fumes</u> from bleach are bad for you. *Fumes* are

   a. harmful gases. **b.** plastic canisters. **c.** dangerous textures.

4. The writer of this blog loves to wear <u>unique</u> clothing. *Unique* means

   a. out of fashion. **b.** mass produced. **c.** one of a kind.

B. Choose a word from the box to complete each sentence.

unique	technique	transform	stencil
consumer	fumes	ventilated	sequence

1. I want to _____ my style so I'm going to make a whole new wardrobe.

2. You may get confused if you follow the steps out of _____ .

3. We applied the _____ to the t-shirt in order to make our own designs.

4. There are many ways to make your own clothes, but stenciling is one _____ that works.

5. On Black Friday you could find me being the typical _____ on line at the mall.

C. Choose three words from the box in Part B. Use each word in a sentence.

1. _____

   _____

2. _____

   _____

3. _____

   _____

© Houghton Mifflin Harcourt Publishing Company

Blog Tips

To continue to evaluate your blog, use the Blog Rubric available from your online Student Resources or from your teacher.

Your Blog

Fill in the boxes to describe your blog.

Purpose	Topic
_____ _____ _____ _____	_____ _____ _____ _____
Audience	**Subscribers**
_____ _____ _____ _____	_____ _____ _____ _____

Blog Post Checklist

Make a mark in the box on the right when you have checked your blog post for each of the following:

1	Is the tone of my blog right for the topic?	
2	Have I checked my spelling and grammar?	
3	Is my language respectful?	
4	Have I been polite to my readers and to anyone I mention in the blog?	
5	Have I checked any facts I include in the blog?	

© Houghton Mifflin Harcourt Publishing Company

Word Families

Use this page to help you with unfamiliar words in "Fashionisto."

creator	consumer	transformation	design	protection

A. Choose a word from the box to answer each question.

1. Which word means "a complete or major change in appearance or form"? _____

2. Which word means "a person who buys goods or services"? _____

3. Which word means "the state of being kept from harm"? _____

4. Which word means "a person who makes something new"? _____

5. Which word means "the visual arrangement of elements and details"? _____

B. Complete the sentences with the correct word from the box. Write it in the space.

1. The _____ of the popular TV series will receive an award tonight.

2. The caterpillar undergoes a complete _____ when it becomes a butterfly.

3. As a _____ I do not like being harassed by salespeople.

4. The terrified witness begged for police _____.

5. Adele fell in love with the _____ of the dress.

C. Write five sentences. Use one word from the box in each sentence.

1. _____

   _____

2. _____

   _____

3. _____

   _____

4. _____

   _____

5. _____

   _____

© Houghton Mifflin Harcourt Publishing Company

Imperative Sentences

A. Circle the imperative sentence.

1. a. Let's go to the store and pick up some chicken thighs.

    b. Go to the store and pick up some chicken thighs.

2. a. Could you please help me carry this?

    b. Please help me carry this.

3. a. If your back hurts, take some medicine.

    b. If your back hurts, you should take some medicine.

4. a. You can't go home without saying goodbye to Mina.

    b. Don't go home without saying goodbye to Mina.

B. Fill in the blanks with an imperative verb.

1. Please _____ a picture of me.

2. Once you get home, _____ me so I know you got there.

3. We can't help you right now, so please _____ again later.

4. _____ on a coat! It's cold.

5. _____ that pencil to me, please.

C. Write four sentences in which you give sequential directions to do something or go somewhere. Possible topics include: cooking, traveling, or making something. All of your sentences should be in the imperative mood.

1. _____

_____

2. _____

_____

3. _____

_____

4. _____

_____

© Houghton Mifflin Harcourt Publishing Company

Information

Answer the questions about *What's In*?

1. What do the kids have to do?

_____

_____

2. What do they decide to focus on?

_____

_____

3. Where did trends used to come from?

_____

_____

4. Where do they come from now?

_____

_____

5. What principles do fashion designers follow?

_____

_____

6. How does Darcy spend a good portion of her time?

_____

_____

Compare and Contrast

Think about the video you have just seen. Compare and contrast it with "Fashionisto."

1. What common theme do the video and the blog share?

_____

_____

2. How are the video and the blog different?

_____

_____

3. If you had to do a report on an aspect of consumer culture, what would you focus it on? Why?

_____

_____

© Houghton Mifflin Harcourt Publishing Company

Build Vocabulary

Critical Vocabulary

A. Circle four words in the Word Bank that you want to know more about.
The words are from the video *What's In?*

Word Bank						
trends	aspects	runway	trickling	primary	destination	principles
brand	inspiration	influence	luxury	retailer	cyclical	accessories

B. Watch the video again and listen for the words. Complete the activity.

1. Word: _____

   What I think it means: _____

   What it means: _____

2. Word: _____

   What I think it means: _____

   What it means: _____

3. Word: _____

   What I think it means: _____

   What it means: _____

4. Word: _____

   What I think it means: _____

   What it means: _____

C. Choose three words that you wrote in Part B. Write a sentence using each word.

1. _____

   _____

2. _____

   _____

3. _____

   _____

© Houghton Mifflin Harcourt Publishing Company

Academic Vocabulary

A. Choose the best description of the attitude displayed by the speaker in each sentence.

curious attitude	friendly attitude	critical attitude

1. That film had amazing special effects; I wonder how it was done. _____

tired attitude	secretive attitude	satisfied attitude

2. Chuck answered my questions with one-word answers. _____

optimistic attitude	aggressive attitude	pessimistic attitude

3. Karen keeps a notebook full of inspiring quotes to share on her blog. _____

B. Complete the answers with information from the text.

> William Shakespeare lived from 1564 to 1616, but his attitude toward women was quite modern. He was a great admirer of Queen Elizabeth I, who was a strong leader, and Shakespeare wrote leading roles for women. His female characters were often described as strong and independent. We can conclude that Shakespeare's attitude was that women could be as skilled at leading as men.

1. How does the writer describe Shakespeare's attitude toward women?

His attitude toward women was _____.

2. How did he demonstrate his attitude about women?

His women characters _____.

3. What can we conclude about Shakespeare's attitude toward women?

He believed that _____.

C. If a friend was very worried about speaking in front of the class, what advice would you give? Write a paragraph about the best attitude to have for speaking in public. Use the words *attitude*, *inspiration* and *influence* in your paragraph.

_____
_____
_____
_____
_____

© Houghton Mifflin Harcourt Publishing Company

Critical Vocabulary

A. Read the sentences below. Circle the definition of each underlined word. Remember that you can look up any unfamiliar words in the dictionary. You can also use context clues to help you figure out word meanings.

1. Brainzilla was <u>mocking</u> Margaret "Cuckoo" Clarke for adopting a strange way of speaking. *Mocking* means

   a. teasing.   **b.** imitating.   **c.** scolding.

2. The king worked hard to make sure his subjects were never <u>deprived</u> of food or shelter. *Deprived* means

   a. working too much.   **b.** wanting to spend money.   **c.** lacking necessities.

3. She feels <u>dingy</u> compared to the well-dressed customers. *Dingy* means

   a. shabby.   **b.** expensive.   **c.** shy.

4. Brainzilla is one of the prettiest girls in school and a total <u>clotheshorse</u>. A *clotheshorse* is a

   a. smart shopper.   **b.** fashionable person.   **c.** popular girl.

B. Choose a word from the box to complete each sentence.

involuntary	carbon monoxide	dingy	deprived	droll	mocking	clotheshorse

1. _____ is a dangerous gas given off by cars and trucks.

2. Her fancy way of speaking about the club was an _____ reflex.

3. The _____ stories about the author's childhood made me laugh out loud.

4. The room was dark and _____, and everything was covered in a layer of dust.

C. Choose three words from the box in Part B. Use each word in a sentence.

1. _____

   _____

   _____

2. _____

   _____

   _____

3. _____

   _____

   _____

© Houghton Mifflin Harcourt Publishing Company

Expressions

make a killing	bug	clotheshorse	short	serious cash

A. Choose a word from the box to answer each question.

1. Which slang expression means "short of money"? _____

2. Which slang expression means "to have great financial success"? _____

3. Which slang expression describes someone who is excessively concerned with buying new clothes? _____

4. Which slang expression means "lots of money"? _____

5. Which slang expression means "to annoy"? _____

B. Complete each sentence with words from the box.

1. My new job will pay _____.

2. My sister, a real _____, goes shopping every day.

3. Mark knew that if he did a good job on the project he would _____.

4. Are you purposely trying to _____ me by asking dumb questions?

5. Because Carmen is always _____, we end up paying for her food.

C. Choose four slang expressions from the box. Use each slang expression in a sentence.

1. _____
   _____

2. _____
   _____

3. _____
   _____

4. _____
   _____

© Houghton Mifflin Harcourt Publishing Company

Sequence of Events

Fill in the chart to indicate the sequence of events in "The Bad Haircut." Review the chart on Student Book p. 211, then fill out this chart in your own words.

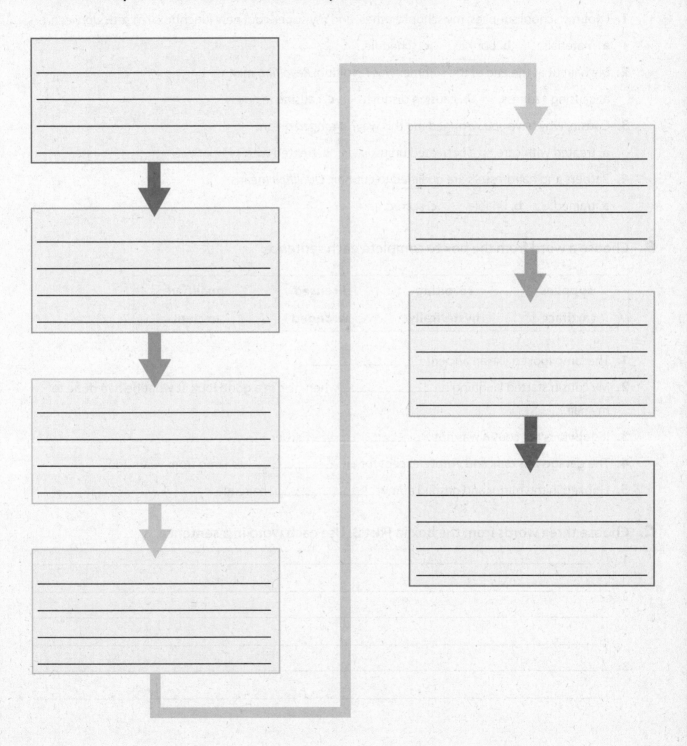

© Houghton Mifflin Harcourt Publishing Company

Critical Vocabulary

A. Read the sentences below. Circle the definition of each underlined word. Remember that you can look up any unfamiliar words in the dictionary.

1. I got my school <u>supplies</u>, my school clothes, and my super-cool new lunchbox. I'm set! *Supplies* are

   a. materials.   **b.** books.   **c.** schedule.

2. My haircut at the end of the summer was <u>revolting</u>. *Revolting* means

   a. causing sadness.   **b.** causing disgust.   **c.** causing jealousy.

3. Cousin, why have you <u>wronged</u> me this way? *Wronged* means

   a. treated with care.   **b.** treated unjustly.   **c.** treated with sympathy.

4. Barbers and hairdressers are <u>qualified</u> to cut hair. *Qualified* means

   a. trained.   **b.** unable.   **c.** scared.

B. Choose a word from the box to complete each sentence.

supplies	revolting	licensed	qualified
artifact	hysterically	wronged	ancient

1. The lamp looked like an ancient _____.

2. My cousin started laughing _____ when he got a good look at what he had done to my hair.

3. It's obvious my cousin was not a _____ barber.

4. The garage was dark and empty, except for an _____ lamp from years ago.

5. I looked in the mirror and gasped at my _____ haircut.

C. Choose three words from the box in Part B. Use each word in a sentence.

1. _____

   _____

2. _____

   _____

3. _____

   _____

© Houghton Mifflin Harcourt Publishing Company

Interrogative Sentences

A. Which word in the sentence asks for information? Circle the correct answer.

1. Where are you spending New Year's Eve?

    a. Where   **b.** you   **c.** are   **d.** Eve

2. Who will drive Lia to the zoo?

    a. to   **b.** will   **c.** Who   **d.** drive

3. How did you finish all that so quickly?

    a. did   **b.** so   **c.** that   **d.** How

4. What did Celia draw?

    a. Celia   **b.** What   **c.** did   **d.** draw

B. Fill in the blanks with a question word.

1. _____ did we elect to lead the group?

2. _____ does Mal look so upset?

3. _____ are you going to solve this problem?

4. _____ does Skylar think about our plans for the day?

5. _____ will you go after school is over?.

C. Choose one topic and write a paragraph about it. Include at least two interrogative sentences in your paragraph. Possible topics:

explain how to cook your favorite meal	say what you would do with a million dollars	explain why something makes you angry

_____

_____

_____

_____

_____

_____

_____

© Houghton Mifflin Harcourt Publishing Company

Collaborative Discussion Support

Use this page to make notes about the lessons Alfonso learned in the podcast.

What did Alfonso *not* think about before getting his haircut?

_____

_____

_____

_____

_____

What effect did getting a free haircut have on Alfonso?

_____

_____

_____

_____

_____

What did the "free" haircut cost Alfonso in things other than money?

_____

_____

_____

_____

_____

How does the old saying "You get what you pay for" apply to Alfonso's situation?

_____

_____

_____

_____

_____

© Houghton Mifflin Harcourt Publishing Company

Academic Vocabulary

A. Complete each sentence with the correct word from the box.

consumer	consume

1. If a product is popular, that means that many people _____ it.

consumerism	consumption

2. The farmer told us that the tomatoes were safe for human _____.

consumerism	consumers

3. Many _____ read online reviews before making major purchases.

consumerism	consumer

4. Some people believe that _____ can be harmful to the environment.

consuming	consumering

5. Bats help humans by _____ between 2,000 and 5,000 insects a night.

B. Complete each sentence.

1. I think people should consume less _____.

2. Consumers buy more when _____.

C. Using a form of *consume,* write a paragraph about three ways you consume energy.

_____

_____

_____

_____

_____

_____

_____

_____

_____

© Houghton Mifflin Harcourt Publishing Company

Critical Vocabulary

A. Read the sentences below. Circle the definition of each underlined word. Remember that you can look up any unfamiliar words in the dictionary.

1. Michelangelo painted the ceiling of the Sistine Chapel with religious figures. A *chapel* is a

   a. building for worship.   **b.** studio for dance.   **c.** castle.

2. The Medicis hired many of Italy's best artisans. *Artisans* are

   a. skilled craftsmen.   **b.** bankers.   **c.** priests.

3. Lorenzo's relationship with Michelangelo was particularly significant. *Particularly* means

   a. usually.   **b.** surprisingly.   **c.** especially.

4. Articles speculate on which works Saatchi will purchase next for his astounding collection. *Astounding* means

   a. commissioned.   **b.** artistic.   **c.** impressive.

B. Choose a word from the box to complete each sentence.

donation	astounding	commissioned	particularly
rebirth	forefront	artisans	chapel

1. The powerful Medici family was at the _____ of the European Renaissance.

2. The government received an impressive _____ from Charles Saatchi's art collection.

3. Artists are often _____ by different organizations to create works of art.

4. The Renaissance was a time period in which art underwent a _____ .

5. The Medicis were _____ known for their love of art.

C. Choose three words from the box in Part B. Use each word in a sentence.

1. _____

   _____

2. _____

   _____

3. _____

   _____

© Houghton Mifflin Harcourt Publishing Company

Collaborative Discussion Support

Part A: Identify Facts

Use the boxes to write down facts about the Medicis. Review Student Book pp. 213–216 and your notes on consumerism.

Cosimo de' Medici	Lorenzo de' Medici
_____	_____
_____	_____
_____	_____
_____	_____
_____	_____
_____	_____
_____	_____

Part B: What Is Art?

Think about why people collect art. How do people decide that something is art, or that it isn't?

What activities can be art?	When are they art?
_____	_____
_____	_____
_____	_____
_____	_____
_____	_____
_____	_____
_____	_____

© Houghton Mifflin Harcourt Publishing Company

Transition Words and Phrases

Part A

In the right column, write transition words that accomplish the purpose noted in the left column.

connect order or time	
compare and contrast	
summarize or conclude	
cause and effect	
add additional detail	
place emphasis	
signal examples	

Part B

Write a line from the text that contains a transitional word or phrase.

_____

_____

Rewrite the line, replacing the transitional word or words.

_____

_____

© Houghton Mifflin Harcourt Publishing Company

Homophones

A. Circle the correct homophone.

1. Which word means "to such a great extent"?

   a. sew   **b.** so

2. Which word means "it is"?

   a. it's   **b.** its

3. Which word means "water that falls in drops from clouds in the sky"?

   a. reign   **b.** rain   **c.** rein

4. Which word means "in that place"?

   a. there   **b.** their   **c.** they're

5. Which word means "the strap attached to the bridle of a horse that is used to guide and control the animal"?

   a. reign   **b.** rain   **c.** rein

B. Complete each sentence with the correct homophone.

1. Put the book over _____. (there, their, they're)

2. The queen's _____ lasted for thirty years. (rain, reign, rein)

3. Maria asked the group to sing her favorite _____. (him, hymn)

4. _____ all going to the party tomorrow night. (There, Their, They're)

5. _____ going to be a great party. (It's, Its)

C. Choose two homophone sets from the box. Use each word in a sentence.

so/sew	its/it's	there/their/they're	rain/reign/rein	him/hymn

1. _____

   _____

   _____

2. _____

   _____

   _____

© Houghton Mifflin Harcourt Publishing Company

Critical Vocabulary

A. Read the sentences below. Circle the definition of each underlined word. Remember that you can look up any unfamiliar words in the dictionary.

1. Walk into any store and you will see the consumption of goods in action. *Consumption* means

   a. taking and using.   **b.** giving up.   **c.** producing.

2. Water is a necessity for life. A *necessity* is

   a. essential.   **b.** easily forgotten.   **c.** optional.

3. A rapacious customer bought all the toys in the store. *Rapacious* means

   a. smart.   **b.** disinterested.   **c.** greedy.

4. Don't let the salesperson manipulate you into buying something you don't want. *Manipulate* means

   a. suggest.   **b.** ask.   **c.** control.

B. Choose a word from the box to complete each sentence.

necessity	undoubtedly	influence	acquire	rapaciously	consumption	desire

1. It is easy to _____ too many things when you go shopping every weekend.

2. Smart phones are _____ a popular product among teenagers.

3. Just because you may _____ something, doesn't mean you need it.

4. Commercials and other ads may _____ our buying habits.

C. Choose three words from the box in Part B. Use each word in a sentence.

1. _____
   _____
   _____

2. _____
   _____
   _____

3. _____
   _____
   _____

© Houghton Mifflin Harcourt Publishing Company

Active and Passive Voice

A. Decide whether each sentence uses the active or passive voice.

1. You and I are Ms. Klug's best students. [active, passive]

2. These clothes were selected with great care. [active, passive]

3. My calls were ignored for two weeks. [active, passive]

4. I need to go out and get some fresh air. [active, passive]

B. Fill in the blanks with a passive verb.

1. You _____ to the party by your mom.

2. This book _____ by a team of several people.

3. The letter _____ via express mail.

4. This fancy coffee _____ by a workers' collective.

5. Vera _____ by her mother and grandmother.

C. Choose one topic and write four sentences about it. Include at least two passive sentences and at least two active sentences in your sentences. Possible topics:

Explain why your favorite kind of pizza is the best.	Talk about a good life motto.	Explain whether you like insects and why or why not.

1. _____

   _____

   _____

2. _____

   _____

   _____

3. _____

   _____

   _____

4. _____

   _____

   _____

© Houghton Mifflin Harcourt Publishing Company

Suffixes –*ly* and –*ness*

widely	regularly	blurriness	sweetness
certainly	enormously	stillness	happiness

A. Choose a word from the box to answer each question.

1. Which word means "of course"? _____

2. Which word means "the quality of being unclear or indistinct"? _____

3. Which word means "at the same time every day, week, month, etc"? _____

4. Which word means "calmness"? _____

5. Which word means "state of well-being, contentment"? _____

B. Complete each sentence with a word from the box.

1. My father was _____ pleased that we planned a surprise party for him.

2. Janelle _____ wanted to know what caused the fire.

3. It has been _____ reported that the crime rate in our town is going down.

4. The _____ of the dessert was pretty overwhelming.

5. Maria's _____ on her wedding day was apparent to everyone who attended the ceremony.

C. Choose five words from the box. Use each word in a sentence.

1. _____

_____

2. _____

_____

3. _____

_____

4. _____

_____

5. _____

_____

© Houghton Mifflin Harcourt Publishing Company

Making an Argument

Read Student Book p. 224 before working on this page.

Claim
Will you or won't you decide to buy a new cell phone you don't need?
_____

Reasons	Evidence
_____	_____
_____	_____
_____	_____
_____	_____
_____	_____

Opposing argument

_____
_____
_____
_____

Counterargument

_____
_____
_____
_____

Concluding sentence

_____
_____
_____
_____

© Houghton Mifflin Harcourt Publishing Company

Build Vocabulary

Academic Vocabulary

A. Complete the answers with information from the text.

> Ever since he first watched a cartoon as a young child, Christian's goal had been to work in animation. As a twelve-year-old, he made a short film about Romeo and Juliet by using two pieces of clay: one blue and one pink. His classmates were impressed by how goal-oriented he was and they weren't surprised when he studied art in college. Finally, he achieved his goal when he got hired as an animator for a famous production studio.

1. What was Christian's goal?

His goal was _____.

2. What was his short film about?

His short film was _____.

3. What were his classmates impressed by?

His classmates were impressed by _____.

4. What was the goal he achieved?

He achieved his goal _____.

B. Complete the sentence starters.

1. When I play _____, my goal is to _____.

2. A goal-oriented person is very _____.

3. My fitness goal is _____.

C. Using the word *goal,* write a paragraph about what you would like to do in the future.

_____

_____

_____

_____

_____

_____

_____

_____

_____

© Houghton Mifflin Harcourt Publishing Company

Analyze Text

Read Student Book pp. 219 and 225 before working on this page.

Vocabulary Strategy

1. What is alliteration?

_____

_____

2. Where are some places you will see alliteration?

_____

_____

3. Do you think alliteration makes things easier to remember? Explain.

_____

_____

4. What else does alliteration do?

_____

_____

5. Rewrite the headline to the advertisement at the beginning of the article, using no alliteration.

_____

_____

6. Which version is more effective?

_____

_____

Analyzing the Text

1. Evaluate

Does the advertisement for earphones make you want to purchase them? _____.

What else would you need to know before you agreed to buy them? _____

2. Analyze

What assumption can you find in the text about advertisements and their influence?

_____

Are there reasons and evidence to support the claims?

_____

© Houghton Mifflin Harcourt Publishing Company

Speak Out!

Write a short presentation with the goal of convincing people that your pen or pencil is something that they absolutely need.

Introductory sentence Make it catchy.	_____ _____ _____ _____ _____ _____ _____ _____
Body Briefly describe the pen or pencil. Use emotional appeal. Make it sound like something everyone needs.	_____ _____ _____ _____ _____ _____ _____ _____
Conclusion What do you want the listener to do?	_____ _____ _____ _____ _____ _____ _____ _____

© Houghton Mifflin Harcourt Publishing Company

Multi-Word Verbs

A. Choose the word or phrase that correctly defines the underlined words.

1. Adam decided to <u>ask around</u> to see how many other students wanted a school newspaper.

   a. ask many people the same question   **b.** have students fill out a form

2. Marlene planned to <u>dress up</u> for the concert.

   a. wear nice clothing   **b.** buy new jeans

3. Jose finally decided to <u>give in</u> and stop arguing.

   a. reluctantly stop arguing   **b.** talk louder

4. Carla suggested that we <u>look up</u> the restaurant's menu on the Internet.

   a. look at a printed copy of something   **b.** search for and find information

5. I hope I <u>come across</u> my lost keys while I'm cleaning.

   a. unexpectedly find   **b.** put in a safe place

B. Complete each sentence with a multi-word verb from the box. Each verb can be used only once.

look up	**ask around**	**give in**
come across	**dress up**	

1. I had to _____ to find out if anyone else wanted to go to the game.

2. To prove how good the pitcher was, Aaron will _____ his pitching record.

3. If you're going to a wedding, you have to _____.

4. Carlotta was determined to win the argument and not to _____.

5. Has anyone _____ my lost wallet?

C. Use two words from the box. Make each verb into a multi-word verb by adding another word to it. Then use each multi-word verb in a sentence.

ask	**come**	**give**	**dress**

1. _____

   _____

2. _____

   _____

© Houghton Mifflin Harcourt Publishing Company

Critical Vocabulary

A. Read the sentences below. Circle the definition of each underlined word. Remember that you can look up any unfamiliar words in the dictionary.

1. In the 1960s there was massive development of <u>infrastructure</u> in Dubai. *Infrastructure* is the

   a. organization of a city. **b.** financial district. **c.** geography.

2. Dubai is an ultramodern city known for its <u>affluence</u>. *Affluence* means

   a. heat. **b.** wealth. **c.** beauty.

3. Burj Khalifa houses <u>luxurious</u> homes and offices. *Luxurious* means

   a. large. **b.** extravagant. **c.** foreign.

4. The Burj Khalifa is an engineering <u>marvel</u>. *Marvel* means

   a. disappointment. **b.** mystery. **c.** wonder.

B. Choose a word from the box to complete each sentence.

symbolic	affluence	rigid	luxurious
marvel	structure	announces	infrastructure

1. Tall towers are _____, but yield to the wind.

2. The _____ of Dubai's buildings are very sound.

3. The Mall of Dubai is _____ of the city's wealth and consumerism.

4. Dubai's downtown area _____ its wealth by its many shops and beautiful buildings.

5. On our vacation to Dubai, we bought many _____ items.

C. Choose three words from the box in Part B. Use each word in a sentence.

1. _____

   _____

2. _____

   _____

3. _____

   _____

© Houghton Mifflin Harcourt Publishing Company

Greek and Latin Roots

Remember that a root is a word part that contains the core meaning of the word. Many English words contain roots that come from older languages, such as Greek and Latin. The words in the box below have either Greek or Latin roots.

telecommunications	architect	elevator
recognized	mega-mall	

A. Choose a word from the box to answer each question.

1. What word means "a person who designs buildings"? _____

2. What word means "a machine used to carry people and things to different levels of a building"? _____

3. What word means "communication over a distance"? _____

4. What word means "a gigantic or huge collection of buildings and stores"? _____

5. What word means "knew that something exists"? _____

B. Complete each sentence with a word from the box.

1. The business firm set up their _____ network in record time.

2. The _____ had every store imaginable.

3. The _____ was stuck on the third floor for fifteen minutes.

4. Alex finally _____ that his cousin was a great athlete.

5. For a solid hour the _____ system was not working.

C. Choose four words from the box. Use each word in a sentence. Write the sentences in the space.

1. _____

2. _____

3. _____

4. _____

© Houghton Mifflin Harcourt Publishing Company

Negative Constructions

A. Decide whether the sentence is affirmative or negative. Circle the correct answer.

1. Griffin made a convincing argument. [affirmative, negative]

2. Jordan didn't want to listen. [affirmative, negative]

3. That seems like a bad idea to me. [affirmative, negative]

4. I couldn't believe it. [affirmative, negative]

B. Fill in the blanks with negative words and verbs to make negative sentences.

1. Simone _____ eating soup.

2. I _____ the movie in theaters, so I'll have to watch it at home.

3. Tom _____ the package he was supposed to mail.

4. Drew _____ to anybody about his poetry.

5. We _____ any more rice.

C. Choose one topic and write four sentences about it. Include at least two negative sentences and at least two affirmative sentences in your paragraph. Make sure to avoid double negatives. Possible topics:

Explain whether you like nature.	something you want to do before you finish high school	if you started a business, what would it do?

1. _____

_____

2. _____

_____

3. _____

_____

4. _____

_____

© Houghton Mifflin Harcourt Publishing Company

Performance Task

Make notes on the chart below that will help you decide whether Joel Sternfeld's quote is supported by evidence in the article. Make notes about examples on the left and facts on the right. Think about which evidence is most relevant and satisfactory. Include that evidence when you present your decision.

> "Dubai is a perfect symbolic site for a consuming world."
> *Joel Sternfeld*

Examples	Facts

© Houghton Mifflin Harcourt Publishing Company

Comparatives and Superlatives

Part A

Read the sentences in the boxes on the left. Change the comparatives to superlatives and the superlatives to comparatives. Then, complete the new sentence in the box on the right.

Original sentence:	New sentence:
The tallest building is Burj Khalifa.	The _____ building is Burj Khalifa.
Sheikh Mohammed asked the architects to build a tower taller than any other building in the world.	Sheikh Mohammed asked the architects to build _____ _____ building in the world.
It features the longest elevator ride and the highest swimming pool in the world.	It features a _____ elevator ride and a _____ swimming pool.
Dubai is filled with the biggest and grandest of everything.	Dubai is filled with _____ and _____ everything.

Part B

How did the meanings of the sentences change when you made the changes?

1. How did the meanings of the sentences change when you made the changes?

    _____

    _____

    _____

2. Write a sentence in which you use comparatives and superlatives to state two facts about something.

    _____

    _____

    _____

© Houghton Mifflin Harcourt Publishing Company

Academic Vocabulary

A. Identify the part of speech for each underlined word.

purchase	purchaser

1. The purchaser asked if she could pay for the groceries with her credit card.

   Part of speech: _____

2. Most families need a loan from the bank to help them purchase a house.

   Part of speech: _____

3. Louis thought his purchase would take about five minutes, but he was in the store for an hour.

   Part of speech: _____

B. Complete each sentence.

1. I should keep the receipts from my purchases because _____

   _____.

2. People sometimes purchase more when they are on vacation because _____

   _____.

C. Use *purchase* or *purchaser* in a paragraph about why you like or don't like to go shopping.

_____

_____

_____

_____

_____

_____

_____

_____

_____

© Houghton Mifflin Harcourt Publishing Company

Build Vocabulary

Critical Vocabulary

Knowing the words below will help you to understand "Great Expectations."

A. Read the sentences below. Circle the definition of each underlined word. Remember that you can look up any unfamiliar words in the dictionary.

1. Miss Havishman was <u>jilted</u> on her wedding day long ago. *Jilted* means

   a. joined.   **b.** wed.   **c.** rejected.

2. Pip begins his <u>apprenticeship</u> as a blacksmith. An *apprenticeship* is a form of

   a. retirement.   **b.** training.   **c.** teaching.

3. Pip wanted to become a <u>gentleman</u> to impress Estella. A *gentleman* is a

   a. lawyer.   **b.** man of good social standing.   **c.** misunderstood man.

4. Pip was miserable and treated even Joe with <u>contempt</u>. *Contempt* means

   a. indifference.   **b.** sympathy.   **c.** scorn.

B. Choose a word from the box to complete each sentence.

jilted	benefactor	amends	disrepair
apprenticeship	gentleman	contempt	anonymous

1. Pip wondered just who his _____ benefactor really was.

2. Miss Havisham's dirty room fell into _____.

3. Pip went to London after being given a large sum of money from a _____.

4. He tried to make _____ with those he had hurt, including Joe.

5. To be a _____ requires socializing with high society.

C. Choose three words from the box in Part B. Use each word in a sentence.

1. _____

   _____

2. _____

   _____

3. _____

   _____

© Houghton Mifflin Harcourt Publishing Company

Compound Words

| churchyard | blacksmith | tombstone | gentleman |
| housekeeper | lifespan | time-consuming | |

A. Choose a word from the box to answer each question.

1. Which word means "a person who makes or repairs things made of iron"? _____

2. Which word means "gravestone"? _____

3. Which word means "a man of high social status"? _____

4. Which word means "a person whose job it is to manage cooking and cleaning"? _____

5. Which means "taking a lot or too much time"? _____

B. Complete each sentence with a word from the box.

1. The average _____ of a tiger is 15 years.

2. In the _____ were many old gravestones.

3. The _____ repaired our iron railing.

4. Reading the entire book will be too _____.

5. The _____ was used to being pampered and waited on.

C. Choose five words from the box. Use each word in a sentence.

1. _____

2. _____

3. _____

4. _____

5. _____

© Houghton Mifflin Harcourt Publishing Company

Collaborative Discussion Support

Use this page to make notes about the main events of the story.

1. What event begins the story? _____
_____
_____

2. What takes Pip away from his sister's home? _____
_____
_____

3. What happens to Pip while he's at Miss Havisham's? _____
_____
_____

4. What takes Pip away from Miss Havisham's? _____
_____
_____

5. What does the lawyer tell Pip? _____
_____
_____

6. What does Pip do during the time he has money? _____
_____
_____

7. What makes Pip confront Miss Havisham? _____
_____

8. Why does Pip go to Egypt? _____
_____
_____

9. When Pip makes his final trip to Miss Havisham's house, what happens? _____
_____
_____

© Houghton Mifflin Harcourt Publishing Company

Visual Clues

The words in the box are from Student Book pp. 233–239.

| convict | captured | bitter | cruel | offended |

A. Choose the best answer from the box to complete each sentence.

1. The _____ old man never got over the fact that his business partner had betrayed him.

2. After a long chase the police finally _____ the thief.

3. Marlena was _____ to learn that her aunt didn't trust her.

4. The _____ youngster took pleasure in making fun of others.

B. Choose the word from the box that most closely defines each of the following descriptions of an illustration. Use the part of speech as a clue.

1. two soldiers pounce on and hold down a struggling man (verb) _____

2. Pip, leaving the house, turns back to look one more time. He looks sad. (noun) _____

3. Estella and Pip are standing on the stairs. Pip looks at her with great fondness. Estella's head is held high, her nose in the air. She looks down on Pip and won't even return his gaze. (adjective) _____

C. Choose three words from the box. Use each word in a sentence that is <u>not</u> about Pip, Estella, or the escaped convict. Write the sentences in the space.

1. _____
   _____
   _____

2. _____
   _____
   _____

3. _____
   _____
   _____

© Houghton Mifflin Harcourt Publishing Company

How English Works

Conjunctive Adverbs

A. **Circle the correct conjunctive adverb to complete the sentence. Circle the correct answer.**

1. It's perfectly safe to bike on this street; _____, it's a shortcut.

   a. next   **b.** finally   **c.** for instance   **d.** furthermore

2. Carlos wins a lot of races; _____, he took first place in the 50-yard dash last week.

   a. in addition   **b.** however   **c.** for example   **d.** as a result

3. A magazine I read was nominated for an award; _____, a different publication won in the end.

   a. however   **b.** for example   **c.** consequently   **d.** next

4. This recipe instructs us to preheat the oven; _____, it says to chop the vegetables.

   a. finally   **b.** next   **c.** however   **d.** as a result

B. **Complete each sentence with a conjunctive adverb.**

1. I feel a little queasy; _____, I'm going home.

2. Dogs scare Annabel; _____, she had to take deep breaths when we passed a golden retriever on the street.

3. Keith worked slowly and focused; _____, he didn't have much editing to do.

4. Most cats don't like water; _____, mine seems to love swimming.

5. I tried to figure out this geometry problem for hours; _____, I realized I needed help.

C. **Choose one topic and write four sentences about it. Include at least two sentences in which independent clauses are joined by conjunctive adverbs. Possible topics:**

something you think is essential for the good life	What kind of mythical creature would you like to be?	What would you do if you encountered an alien?

1. _____

2. _____

3. _____

4. _____

© Houghton Mifflin Harcourt Publishing Company

Analyzing the Text Support

Review "Great Expectations," and the questions on p. 241 of the Student Book to answer the questions below.

Interpret	
When Miss Havisham asks Pip whether he would like to see Estella again, he responds by saying, "Y-y-yes, Miss Havisham." What does the repeating of the letter *y* tell you about how Pip is feeling?	_____ _____ _____ _____ _____ _____ _____

Infer	
What can we infer about Joe, Pip's brother-in-law, from the way he treats Pip?	_____ _____ _____ _____ _____ _____ _____

Compare and Contrast	
How do Pip's feelings about being rich change throughout the story?	_____ _____ _____ _____ _____ _____

© Houghton Mifflin Harcourt Publishing Company

Idioms

| paint the town | slap on the wrist | add fuel to the fire |
| a piece of cake | down to the wire | |

A. Choose the correct idiom from the box to answer each question.

1. Which idiom means "to celebrate or party"? _____

2. Which idiom describes a task that can be done very easily? _____

3. Which idiom means "a very mild punishment"? _____

4. Which idiom means "to make a bad situation worse"? _____

5. Which idiom means "something that ends or is finished at the last minute"?

   _____

B. Complete each sentence with an idiom from the box.

1. After learning that he had landed the new job, Enrico decided to _____.

2. Oh, don't worry. Fixing your bike will be _____.

3. Even though Dan had purposely destroyed property, the punishment he was given

   was _____.

4. If you continue to argue you'll just _____.

5. Getting the project in on time went _____.

C. Choose three idioms from the box at the top of the page. Use each idiom in a sentence.

1. _____

   _____

2. _____

   _____

3. _____

   _____

© Houghton Mifflin Harcourt Publishing Company

Written Argument Topics

Choose three of the selections from this unit to write about (see the list below).
Read all of Student Book p. 242 to complete this page.

"Fashionisto"

"The Bad Haircut"

"The Medicis: Consumers of Art"

"Want vs. Need"

"Dubai: Going to Extremes"

"Great Expectations"

_____

_____

_____

_____

_____

_____

_____

_____

_____

Write three possible topics for your written argument.

Idea 1 _____

_____

_____

Idea 2 _____

_____

_____

Idea 3 _____

_____

_____

© Houghton Mifflin Harcourt Publishing Company

Plan Your Written Argument

To evaluate your written argument, use the Written Argument Rubric available from your online Student Resources or from your teacher.

State Your Claim

Write your claim as a statement. You might expand on it with an interesting fact or thought-provoking question.

_____

_____

Find Reasons

What reasons, facts, and opinions from the selections can you use?

_____

_____

What reasons, facts, and opinions from other sources could you use?

_____

_____

What opposing claims (other points of view) might you address?

_____

_____

Know Your Sources

Which credible sources will you use?

_____

_____

Think About Style

What transitional and time-order words and phrases might you use?

_____

_____

Which technical or unfamiliar words should you explain?

_____

_____

© Houghton Mifflin Harcourt Publishing Company

Academic Vocabulary

A. Complete each sentence with the correct word from the box.

technologies	technologically

1. I enjoy reading science fiction stories about _____ advanced alien species.

technological	technologic

2. Our lives are filled with _____ devices that can be convenient as well as distracting.

technology	technologically

3. Some department stores use _____ to instantly see if they have the color and size of the shoe you want.

B. Complete each sentence.

1. An example of a technological device that I use everyday is _____.

2. The latest technological news I have heard is that _____.

C. Write a paragraph using at least two words from the box about a technological problem you have experienced.

technology	technological	technologically

_____
_____
_____
_____
_____
_____
_____
_____
_____
_____

© Houghton Mifflin Harcourt Publishing Company

Finalize Your Plan

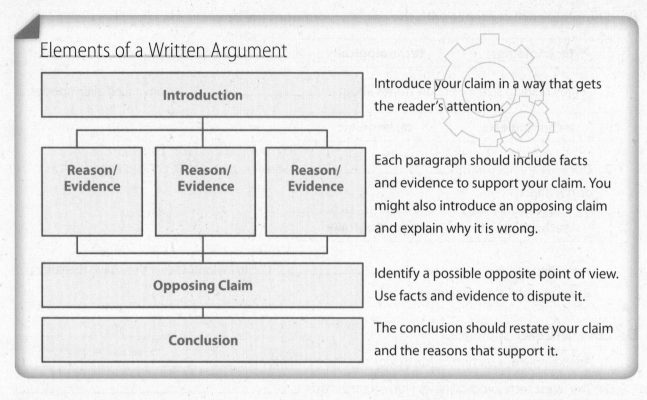

Elements of a Written Argument

Introduction — Introduce your claim in a way that gets the reader's attention.

Reason/Evidence · **Reason/Evidence** · **Reason/Evidence** — Each paragraph should include facts and evidence to support your claim. You might also introduce an opposing claim and explain why it is wrong.

Opposing Claim — Identify a possible opposite point of view. Use facts and evidence to dispute it.

Conclusion — The conclusion should restate your claim and the reasons that support it.

A. Review the elements of a written argument above. Describe the elements that you will include in your argument.

Introduction _____

_____

Reasons/Evidence _____

_____

Opposing Claim _____

_____

Conclusion _____

_____

B. Write a brief summary of your argument.

_____

_____

_____

_____

© Houghton Mifflin Harcourt Publishing Company

Vocabulary Review

Here are some of the words you learned in this unit. Choose words from this list and sort them into the categories below. There are many possible correct answers.

acquire	consumption	manipulate	technique
apprenticeship	disrepair	purchaser	technologically
architect	donation	qualified	telecommunications
artifact	enormously	rapaciously	tombstone
astounding	fumes	recognized	transform
attitude	gentleman	sequence	unique
blacksmith	happiness	sew	ventilated
certainly	him	so	widely
churchyard	housekeeper	stencil	
consume	hysterically	stillness	
consumer	lifespan	sweetness	

Homophone Pairs

1. _____

   _____

2. _____

   _____

Words with Suffixes

1. _____
2. _____
3. _____
4. _____
5. _____

Compound Words

1. _____
2. _____
3. _____
4. _____
5. _____

Nouns

1. _____
2. _____
3. _____
4. _____
5. _____

© Houghton Mifflin Harcourt Publishing Company

Easily Confused Words

buy	bye	buy	affect	effect

A. Circle the correct word in each sentence. Use context clues to help you decide which word is correct.

  1. I try not to [by, bye, buy] too many clothes I don't need.

  2. What was the [affect, effect] of changing the amount of salt in the recipe?

  3. After school, let's go [by, bye, buy] the movie theater and see what's showing.

  4. Lee worries that spending time after school at play rehearsals might [affect, effect] his grades.

B. Complete each sentence with the correct word from the box.

  1. We need to _____ some eggs so we can make meringue.

  2. _____! Have a nice trip!

  3. This novel is _____ the same author as some other very popular ones.

  4. I don't know what _____ changing school hours would have on students.

  5. Caffeine can _____ you very strongly if you don't use it often.

C. Write four sentences, two using *by, bye,* or *buy* and two using *affect* or *effect*. Your sentences should demonstrate your understanding of the meaning of each word.

What would you do if you could travel wherever you wanted for a month?	What would you say to a million people?	What famous people would you want to be related to?

  1. _____

   _____

  2. _____

   _____

  3. _____

   _____

  4. _____

   _____

© Houghton Mifflin Harcourt Publishing Company

Guided by a Cause

"Know what you want to do,

hold the thought firmly,

and do every day what should be done,

and every sunset will see you

that much nearer the goal."

— Elbert Hubbard, author

What do you think of when you imagine yourself or another person working for a cause? Draw pictures or write your thoughts below.

Describe some causes you believe in. Also describe causes for which friends and people in your family have worked.

_____

_____

_____

Record other notes about people who have worked hard to achieve important goals that benefit others.

_____

_____

_____

© Houghton Mifflin Harcourt Publishing Company

Academic Vocabulary

As you work through Unit 6, look and listen for these words. Use them when you talk in class and in your writing. Write about your experiences using these words in the last column of the chart.

Word	Definition	Related Forms	My Experiences
contrast	• to compare people or things to show how they are different • difference	contrasting contrasted	
despite	in spite of; even though		
error	a mistake	err, erroneous, erroneously	
inadequate	not enough or not good enough	adequate, adequately, inadequately adequacy, inadequacy	
interact	to act upon each other	interaction, interactive	

© Houghton Mifflin Harcourt Publishing Company

Turning Adjectives Into Action: Suffix –*ly*

Adverb	Meaning
bravely	"in a courageous way"
defiantly	"in a resistant way"
eagerly	"in an extremely interested way"
proudly	"in a way that shows satisfaction with self-worth"
successfully	"in a successful way that meets all requirements"
victoriously	"in a triumphant way"

Complete each sentence with an adverb from the chart above. You will need to use two of the adverbs twice.

1. After _____ completing our project, we turned it in and received an A for content and an A+ for presentation.

2. The woman _____ refused to obey laws that she considered unjust.

3. Standing onstage with the other winners, Julie _____ received her medal for leadership and high grades.

4. I had been waiting for this package to arrive for at least a month! I _____ ripped off the tape, opened the box, and gazed at my beautiful new shoes.

5. After winning the state soccer championship, we raced gleefully and _____ around the field. "We're Number One!" we screamed.

6. The knight _____ faced the horrible monster, defeating it before it could eat anymore of the townspeople's cows and sheep.

7. On the night of the concert we waited _____ in line to see our favorite band, and it was worth the long wait—they *rocked*!

8. After I have _____ completed middle school, I hope to attend the same high school that my brother and sister attend.

© Houghton Mifflin Harcourt Publishing Company

Letter About a Cause

Read the Performance Task directions on Student Book p. 249 to complete this page.

A. Plan Your Letter

1. What cause will you write about? Reread page 249 in your **Student Book** and look through the articles in *Browse* magazine to help you think of ideas. Write the names of three causes that are meaningful to you—ones that you can imagine supporting with your time and effort:

    a. _____

    b. _____

    c. _____

    After thinking it over, circle the cause you will write about in your letter.

2. Take some notes about this cause.

    a. How would you describe this cause in a few phrases? _____

    _____

    b. Does this cause have to do with politics, a charity, the environment, or animals? [Circle one]

    If it has do with something else record it here. _____

    _____

    c. What is honorable about this cause? Who does it help, or what problem does it attempt to solve?

    _____

B. Write Your Letter Use the details you wrote in Part A to write your letter on another sheet of paper. Study the letter format example below and remember to include: the date; a greeting; the body of your letter, which can be two to five paragraphs long, but should not be longer than one page; a closing; and a signature.

Letter Format

November 26, 2015 ◀ **date**

Dear Editor of the *Alameda Daily News*: ◀ **greeting**

Here is the first paragraph of the body of my letter. It tells what I am writing for. ◀ **body**
Here is the second paragraph of the body of my letter. It adds important details and information.
Here is the last paragraph of the body of my letter. In conclusion, thanks for reading my letter.

Yours truly, ◀ **closing**
Maxwell Rex Ramirez ◀ **signature**

© Houghton Mifflin Harcourt Publishing Company

Collaborative Discussion Support

Reread the blog "DogGone" and answer the questions in the chart below.

Questions	My Answers
1. What information does the blogger discover by doing Internet research on adopting a dog?	
2. If you were adopting a pet, what sources would you use to find information? Mention both books and Internet sources.	
3. What words and phrases would you use as search terms or topics in indexes?	
4. What words, phrases, and sentences in the blog show that the blogger is excited about her new dog?	
5. What are some ways to talk about places without giving specific locations?	

© Houghton Mifflin Harcourt Publishing Company

Critical Vocabulary

A. Read the sentences from the blog "DogGone." Circle the definition of each underlined word. Remember that you can look up any unfamiliar words in the dictionary.

1. I've been asking, <u>nagging</u>, <u>begging</u> my parents to let me get a dog. *Nagging* means

   a. bothering.   **b.** suggesting.   **c.** saying.

2. *Begging* means

   a. following up.   **b.** asking emotionally.   **c.** answering.

3. Adopting a shelter dog means I'm getting a dog, just like I wanted, AND doing a great thing for my <u>canine</u> friends. *Canine* means

   a. horse.   **b.** dog.   **c.** French.

4. After school today, Mom and I went shopping for a <u>crate</u> with a nice cushion in it. *Crate* means

   a. dog seat.   **b.** big sack.   **c.** box.

B. Choose a word from the box to complete each sentence.

nagging	shelters	begging	canine	adopting	crate

1. Many people go to shelters hoping to find a _____ companion.

2. After the hurricane, volunteers collected lost pets and took them to _____ .

3. The scientists observed the cat _____ a motherless piglet and letting it feed with her kittens.

4. The zookeepers were unpacking a kangaroo from its traveling _____ .

C. Choose three words from the box in **Part B**. Use each word in a sentence.

1. _____

   _____

2. _____

   _____

3. _____

   _____

© Houghton Mifflin Harcourt Publishing Company

Write Text for a Persuasive Poster

Read Student Book p. 252 before working on this page.

A. Plan Your Poster

1. What images (photos or illustrations) might you put on your poster? _____
_____

2. Take notes on some important persuasive ideas you want to express on your poster.

_____
_____
_____
_____

B. Write Text for Your Poster Use your Part A notes to write your poster text below. Remember:

1. Your poster should be persuasive, but it should not make people feel guilty.

2. Give reasons that explain why adopting a shelter pet is a good thing to do.

3. Try to make your readers feel excited about adopting a shelter pet. Give reasons why animals make our lives happier and healthier.

4. Sum up your ideas in your last phrase or sentence.

_____
_____
_____
_____
_____
_____
_____
_____

© Houghton Mifflin Harcourt Publishing Company

Share and Interact with Other Blogs

Write down as many ideas as you can in response to the questions below. Be sure to follow class safety guidelines while interacting with other bloggers.

What are the names of some of the blogs you like? (If you can't think of the exact names, write down the blogs' topics.) Tell whether you have commented on these blogs.

_____

_____

_____

Now search for some new blogs to read. What search terms will you use? (Hint: Searching for *blogs on dogs or blogs on cats* will lead you to thousands of blog sites.)

_____

_____

_____

What are the names of the new blogs you found that you like? Have you commented on any of those blogs' posts? Have you shared links to your blog?

_____

_____

_____

Which of your blog posts do you want readers to comment on? How will you encourage people to comment? Have you asked your readers to suggest more topics for you to blog about? What topics did they suggest?

_____

_____

_____

Now that you have interacted with other bloggers, tell about your experiences. Are you making sure not to share personal information about yourself and where you live?

_____

_____

_____

© Houghton Mifflin Harcourt Publishing Company

Build Vocabulary

Multiple-Meaning Words

shelter	check	canine	wear	patient

A. Circle the response that correctly defines the underlined word. All of the words in the box are taken from the selection "DogGone."

1. To make sure that his dog was healthy, Ryan would <u>check</u> his spaniel for fleas every day.

   a. inspect   **b.** restrain

2. When teaching a dog to "sit" or "stay," the pet owner needs to be <u>patient</u>.

   a. a person receiving medical treatment   **b.** understanding, willing to take time

3. When Randall found a poodle wandering on the street, he took the dog to a <u>shelter</u>.

   a. protect   **b.** a place that cares for stray pets

4. Peanut butter is a favorite <u>canine</u> food, and it's actually healthy for dogs.

   a. tooth   **b.** relating to dogs

5. Stacy felt confident she could <u>wear</u> down her mother's resistance to getting a dog.

   a. overcome by persisting   **b.** dress in

B. Define each underlined word.

1. A dentist will tell you that <u>canines</u> are sharp and used to grip and tear food. _____

2. The sudden rainstorm surprised the class on their picnic, and the students had to take <u>shelter</u> inside the park's visitor center. _____

3. The big dog was snarling and barking, but luckily was <u>checked</u> by the owner's firm hold on its collar. _____

4. Some special dogs have such a healing effect that they may even visit a <u>patient</u> in the hospital.

   _____

5. In cold weather, many people like to <u>wear</u> several layers of clothes to keep warm.

   _____

C. Choose a word from the box. Use the word in two sentences that show different meanings of the word.

Sentence: _____

_____

Sentence: _____

_____

© Houghton Mifflin Harcourt Publishing Company

Dangling Modifiers and Misplaced Modifiers

A. Decide how to correct each sentence. Circle the correct answer.

1. I went up to the girl with the long hair from my English class.

  a. I went up to the girl with the long hair in my English class.

  b. I went up to the long-haired girl from my English class.

2. Her brother bought a new car from a friend with lots of trunk space.

  a. Her brother bought with lots of trunk space a new car from a friend.

  b. Her brother bought a new car with lots of trunk space from a friend.

3. Walking home, my neighbor waved at me from her porch.

  a. While I was walking home, my neighbor waved at me from her porch.

  b. I was walking home, my neighbor waved at me from her porch.

4. On arriving at the store, Kulap's wallet was missing.

  a. Kulap's wallet, on arriving at the store, was missing.

  b. When Kulap arrived at the store, her wallet was missing.

B. Complete each sentence with an independent clause. Be careful to avoid dangling modifiers.

1. While brushing my hair, _____.

2. _____ under the sink.

3. Having finished the whole package, _____.

4. _____ behind the couch.

5. Paying close attention to the presentation, _____.

C. Choose one topic and write a paragraph about it. Include at least three modifier phrases in your paragraph, and make sure to avoid dangling or misplaced modifiers. Possible topics:

describe a purchase you made recently	explain how to break bad news to someone	describe something you find very beautiful

_____

_____

_____

_____

© Houghton Mifflin Harcourt Publishing Company

Cause and Effect

A. Answer the questions about *A Special Horse Farm*.

1. Where do the events in the video take place? (What is the setting?)

   _____

2. What cause is served by this special work farm?

   _____

3. What effect does working with the horses have on people with disabilities?

   _____

4. What activities do people with disabilities do with the horses?

   _____

5. How can people help the TEC?

   _____

Compare and Contrast

B. Think about the video you have just seen. Compare and contrast it with "DogGone."

1. What common theme do the video and the blog share?

   _____

   _____

   _____

   _____

2. How are the video and the blog different?

   _____

   _____

   _____

   _____

3. Would you rather visit an animal shelter or the special horse farm from the video? Why?

   _____

   _____

   _____

   _____

© Houghton Mifflin Harcourt Publishing Company

Critical Vocabulary

A. Circle four words in the Word Bank that you want to know more about. All the words are taken from *A Special Horse Farm.*

> ### Word Bank
>
> | | | | |
> |---|---|---|---|
> | therapeutic | barriers | client | mimic |
> | equestrian | equine | props | gait |

B. Watch the video again and listen for the words. Use context clues and what you know about the words you've chosen to write what you think each word means. Next, look the words up in a dictionary and see how close you came to the meaning.

1. Word: _____

What I think it means: _____

What it means: _____

2. Word: _____

What I think it means: _____

What it means: _____

3. Word: _____

What I think it means: _____

What it means: _____

4. Word: _____

What I think it means: _____

What it means: _____

C. Choose three words that you wrote in Part B. Write a sentence using each word.

1. _____

_____

2. _____

_____

3. _____

_____

© Houghton Mifflin Harcourt Publishing Company

Academic Vocabulary

A. Read the passage and answer the questions.

> On the chilly morning of the race, the sun shined bright, in contrast to last year's rainy day. Jane didn't mind the cold. Mary, on the other hand, presented a contrasting attitude, grumbling as she ran. Later, at the finish line, the announcer contrasted the attitudes of the runners as they crossed—one cool and calm, while the other waved her arms and gasped for air.

1. Why was the weather a contrast from last year's race?

The sun was bright, but last year it was a _____.

2. How did Jane's attitude contrast with Mary's?

Jane didn't mind the cold, but Mary was _____.

3. How did the announcer contrast the runners' attitudes?

The announcer noted that one was cool and calm while the other _____
_____.

B. Complete each sentence.

1. Chiles are spicy; in contrast, pineapple _____
_____.

2. In cold weather, people usually wear layers of clothes to keep warm. In contrast, on hot summer days people often wear _____
_____.

C. Write two sentences contrasting a sunny day and a rainy day using a form of *contrast*.

1. _____
_____
_____
_____

2. _____
_____
_____
_____

© Houghton Mifflin Harcourt Publishing Company

Critical Vocabulary

A. **Read the sentences below. Circle the definition of each underlined word. Remember that you can look up any unfamiliar words in the dictionary.**

1. No one told the youngsters about the city's segregation laws for buses. *Segregation* means

   a. opposition. **b.** separation. **c.** universal.

2. One day they boarded a bus and sat down by a white man and boy. *Boarded* means

   a. rode on top of. **b.** faced. **c.** got on.

3. The driver called the police, and Edwina and Marshall were arrested. *Arrested* means

   a. taken to jail. **b.** judged. **c.** proven guilty.

4. Up North, they were accustomed to riding integrated buses and trains. *Integrated* means

   a. open route. **b.** not separated. **c.** large, clean.

B. **Choose a word from the box to complete each sentence.**

segregation	arrested	boarded	convicted	integrated	entitled

1. The Bill of Rights tells some of the rights that Americans are _____ to have.

2. The whole soccer team _____ the bus one by one.

3. When people are _____ of crimes, a judge decides their punishment.

4. _____ became illegal in the United States in 1954.

C. **Choose three words from the box in Part B. Use each word in a sentence.**

1. _____

   _____

   _____

2. _____

   _____

   _____

3. _____

   _____

   _____

© Houghton Mifflin Harcourt Publishing Company

Collaborative Discussion Support

Follow the Collaborative Discussion directions on page 259 of the Student Book.

A. Reread "Claudette Colvin." Complete the following timeline about events in a chronological (time) order.

In 1949, Edwina and Marshall Johnson are arrested for refusing to give up their seats on a Montgomery bus.	On March 2, 1955, Claudette Colvin _____	The bus fills up, so people have to _____	The driver stops the bus and tells _____

The policemen _____	After Claudette refuses, the driver _____	Claudette is now alone on a double seat. The driver _____	The driver even tells a pregnant black woman to _____

Claudette is in jail until _____	In court, Claudette is charged with both _____

B. Be sure to include line numbers and page numbers for each quotation.

page/lines	Quotation from Claudette Colvin	What the Quote Tells Us About Claudette's Beliefs, Traits, and Feelings

© Houghton Mifflin Harcourt Publishing Company

Practice for an Oral Presentation

A. Plan Your Presentation

1. Fill in the following chart with your opinions about the events. You do not have to write in complete sentences. Remember to include both main ideas and details.

2. Carefully review the notes you wrote in the chart.

Events in "Claudette Colvin"	My Opinions About the Events (Including Reasons for My Opinions)
the arrest of Edwina and Marshall Johnson in 1949	
Claudette's actions on March 2, 1955	
the bus driver's actions on March 2, 1955	
the policemen's actions on March 2, 1955	
Claudette's trial	

B. Practice Your Presentation

As you practice with your partner, remember to:

- Make your presentation fairly short. (Two to three minutes is long enough.)

- Speak slowly and clearly, but not *too* slowly. Make sure your partner can understand every word you say.

- You will probably need to look down at your notes, but look up often.

- Express your ideas with feeling. (If you feel angry about some of the events, it is fine to show it, as long as you don't yell.)

- Look at your listener and give him or her a chance to react to what you are saying—your partner might do so by nodding, smiling, frowning, and/or gesturing.

© Houghton Mifflin Harcourt Publishing Company

Specialized Vocabulary

segregation	convicted	hearing	bail	battery	constitutional

A. Choose the correct word from the box to answer each question.

1. What word describes a system that requires separate facilities (such as schools or housing) based on race or ethnicity? _____

2. What word means to get someone out of jail temporarily by paying a sum of money for their release? _____

3. What word is a legal term for beating or striking another person? _____

4. What word refers to rights or rules listed in a country's founding legal document? _____

5. What is the word given to a legal proceeding which considers evidence and arguments for charging someone with a crime? _____

B. Complete each sentence with the correct word from the box.

1. The jurors found him guilty, and he was _____ of the crime of shoplifting.

2. Except in a few instances, freedom of speech is a _____ right that cannot be taken away by law.

3. After her arrest, Christine's friends raised the $1000 _____ money needed to get her released from jail.

4. In 1954 the Supreme Court ruled that _____ in schools was illegal, and black students began to attend schools that had been all-white.

5. The judge held a _____ to decide whether there was enough evidence to order a trial of the accused person.

C. Choose three words from the box. Use each word in a sentence.

1. _____

   _____

2. _____

   _____

3. _____

   _____

© Houghton Mifflin Harcourt Publishing Company

Sequence of Events in the Podcast

As you listen to the podcast, fill in the missing parts of the timeline. When you're finished, compare your chart to the one in the Student Book on p. 261.

Tim King's parents give him a privileged childhood. They raise him to get a college and law school education and want him to become president of the United States.

After law school, Tim deviates from this plan by _____

Tim becomes close to a student named Keith, who stays late at school and asks _____

Keith calls Tim from his cold and unlit apartment the night his mother dies of a drug overdose.

Tim helps Keith _____

Keith asks Tim if _____

Tim agrees, even though _____

The two of them find it hard to live together at first.

Keith goes on to college and becomes _____

Tim is touched when Keith texts him because _____

© Houghton Mifflin Harcourt Publishing Company

Critical Vocabulary

A. Read the sentences below. Circle the definition of each underlined word. Remember that you can look up any unfamiliar words in the dictionary.

1. One night, I got a call from Keith, and he was in <u>hysterics</u>. *Hysterics* means

   a. a rare position.   **b.** difficulties.   **c.** a panic.

2. Now he works with me at a <u>network</u> of charter public high schools that I started called Urban Prep. *Network* means

   a. system.   **b.** library.   **c.** one single part.

3. Keith was <u>berating</u> me about missing the basketball game. *Berating* means

   a. scolding.   **b.** battering.   **c.** explaining to.

4. <u>Eventually</u>, the summer melted into the school year. *Eventually* means

   a. quickly.   **b.** finally.   **c.** happily.

B. Choose a word from the box to complete each sentence.

elaborate	network	upbringing	berating	hysterics	eventually

1. The Underground Railroad was actually a _____ of people who wanted to help slaves gain their freedom.

2. June's _____ on a farm involved a lot of hard work taking care of animals.

3. My family celebrates Chinese New Year with an _____ dinner with a lot of relatives and guests.

4. The mother duck was in _____ because her little duckling just couldn't seem to swim straight.

C. Choose three words from the box in Part B. Use each word in a sentence.

1. _____

   _____

2. _____

   _____

3. _____

   _____

© Houghton Mifflin Harcourt Publishing Company

Two-Way Modifiers and Misplaced Clauses

A. Decide how to correct each sentence. Circle the correct answer.

1. The athletes who ran quickly improved.

    a. The athletes quickly who ran improved.

    b. The athletes who ran improved quickly.

2. You told me earlier today you were working on biology homework.

    a. Earlier today, you told me you were working on biology homework.

    b. You told me you were working on earlier today biology homework.

3. Here's the document I got from Jan that needs editing.

    a. Here's the document I got that needs editing from Jan.

    b. Here's the document that needs editing I got from Jan.

4. Sebastian took the bag from the customer that needed repairing.

    a. Sebastian took the bag that needed repairing from the customer.

    b. Sebastian took that needed repairing the bag from the customer.

B. Complete each sentence with an independent clause. Be careful to avoid misplaced modifiers.

1. _____ who answered the question _____.

2. _____ that she found.

3. _____ with the red hair _____.

4. _____ which Sara drew last week.

5. _____ who opened the door slowly _____.

C. Choose one topic and write a paragraph about it. Include at least two modifier phrases and at least two modifier clauses in your paragraph, and make sure to avoid any modifier errors. Possible topics:

describe a game you like and why it's so great	describe something fun you used to do when you were little	explain something you learned this week

_____

_____

_____

_____

© Houghton Mifflin Harcourt Publishing Company

Collaborative Discussion Support

Listen to the podcast for the third time. Use the organizer to retell the story in your own words.

In the beginning of his talk, Tim King tells about

_____
_____
_____
_____
_____
_____

The middle of Tim's talk tells how Tim becomes close to a student named Keith, who

_____
_____
_____
_____
_____
_____
_____
_____
_____
_____
_____
_____

Tim ends his talk by telling about:

_____
_____
_____
_____
_____

© Houghton Mifflin Harcourt Publishing Company

Academic Vocabulary

A. Write *despite, despite himself,* or *despite ourselves* to complete the following sentences.

1. He took the book from his friend's locker without asking, _____.

2. Marni's answer is correct, _____ what you might think.

3. During the baseball game, we sat outside in the rain _____.

4. _____ the crowds, Joaquin still got a table in the busy restaurant.

B. Complete the sentences.

1. Despite having studied all night, Bailey _____
   _____
   _____.

2. Despite Josie's bad experience the first time she went horseback riding, she _____
   _____
   _____.

3. Despite his stage fright, Derek _____.

C. Using *despite* or *despite the fact*, write about something you have achieved after overcoming an obstacle.

_____
_____
_____
_____
_____
_____
_____
_____
_____
_____
_____
_____

© Houghton Mifflin Harcourt Publishing Company

Critical Vocabulary

A. Read the sentences below. Circle the definition of each underlined word. Remember that you can look up any unfamiliar words in the dictionary.

1. For more than eight hours, thirteen-year-old Cesar had been <u>toiling</u> under the burning rays of the sun. *Toiling* means

   a. laboring.   **b.** collecting.   **c.** painting.

2. His back <u>ached</u> from stooping to reach the fat bunches of grapes that hung low on the <u>vines</u>. *Ached* means

   a. was insensitive.   **b.** was broken.   **c.** was sore.

3. *Vines* means

   a. branches.   **b.** climbing plants.   **c.** horizon.

4. They would put in a day's work tomorrow, <u>attempt</u> to collect what they were owed, and be on their way. *Attempt* means

   a. try.   **b.** demand.   **c.** practice.

B. Choose a word from the box to complete each sentence.

toiling	contractor	ached	attempt	vines	jug

1. The family hired a _____ to fix up their house, and she hired the construction workers.

2. When people go on a picnic, they often take along a big _____ of lemonade or water.

3. Dinesh wanted to build his tree house in one day, but after three hours his arms _____ from carrying boards.

4. He decided to rest until tomorrow and _____ to finish it then.

C. Choose three words from the box in Part B. Use each word in a sentence.

1. _____

   _____

2. _____

   _____

3. _____

   _____

© Houghton Mifflin Harcourt Publishing Company

Compound Words

Remember that compound words are two or more words that are used together to form a new word with a new meaning.

| farmworkers | storytelling | extraordinary | vineyard | backbreaking | smooth-talking |

A. Choose a word from the box to answer each question.

1. Which word means "demanding great physical effort"? _____

2. Which word means "a tract of land where grapes are grown"? _____

3. Which word means "relating tales"? _____

4. Which word means "people who labor at growing food"? _____

5. Which means "unusual"? _____

6. Which word means "speaking in a pleasant but misleading way"? _____

B. Complete each sentence with a word from the box.

1. The _____ computer salesman convinced us to buy a printer that uses up ink faster than a thirsty dog drinks water.

2. The Rubired variety of grapes is the only kind grown on the _____ we toured.

3. Some _____ service dogs can turn on lights and open doors for owners who aren't able to do these tasks themselves.

4. The first union agreement between vineyard owners and _____ in the continental U.S. was signed in 1966.

5. Shoveling snow can be _____ work, which is probably why snowblowers were invented.

6. In Mexico, grandmothers often teach children, as well as entertaining them, through _____.

C. Choose three words from the box. Use each word in a sentence.

1. _____

_____

2. _____

_____

3. _____

_____

© Houghton Mifflin Harcourt Publishing Company

Critical Vocabulary

A. Read the sentences below. Circle the definition of each underlined word. Remember that you can look up any unfamiliar words in the dictionary.

1. A young girl was <u>sweeping</u> the floor of her mother's hotel in Stockton, California. *Sweeping* means

   a. mopping.   **b.** pacing.   **c.** brushing clean.

2. "Dolores! Come here!" Mama <u>summoned</u>. *Summoned* means

   a. called her to come.   **b.** was thinking.   **c.** said.

3. Dolores guessed that they probably wouldn't pay what they owed for <u>lodging</u> that week. *Lodging* means

   a. breakfast.   **b.** rented rooms.   **c.** the plants.

4. <u>Chores</u> were plentiful and constant, and the children's help was instrumental to keeping the hotel going. *Chores* means

   a. changes.   **b.** housework.   **c.** customers.

B. Choose a word from the box to complete each sentence.

sweeping	lodging	broom	wage	summoned	chores

1. After we finish _____ the floor with the _____, we mop it.

2. When we go on vacation, we spend more money on _____ than on meals and transportation.

3. The principal _____ two boys to the office to give them a message.

4. Many workers in offices and stores get paid an hourly _____ .

C. Choose three words from the box in Part B. Use each word in a sentence.

1. _____

   _____

2. _____

   _____

3. _____

   _____

© Houghton Mifflin Harcourt Publishing Company

Wordiness

A. Circle the answer that correctly restates the information in the sentence.

1. At a later date, Leticia stated that she went home due to the fact that she was tired.

   a. Later, Leticia stated that she went home because she was tired.

   b. Later, Leticia stated that she went home due to she was tired.

2. I like the tea that is made of apples.

   a. I like the tea that apples.

   b. I like the apple tea.

3. She goes to a school that is considered very prestigious.

   a. She goes to a very prestigious school.

   b. She goes very prestigious to school.

4. In my personal opinion, there are too few people working to fight poverty.

   a. In my personal opinion, too few people are working to fight poverty.

   b. In my opinion, too few people are working to fight poverty.

B. Rewrite the sentences to make them less wordy.

1. The end result of our procedures was a solution that has a tendency to turn an orange color.

_____

_____

2. By virtue of the fact that it does not seem like an appealing job, there are not many people applying to become the class monitor.

_____

_____

C. Choose one topic and write a paragraph about it. Go into as much depth as you can with the smallest number of words. Possible topics:

something that you discovered recently that you're excited about	a new development in technology	something more people should try to do

_____

_____

_____

_____

© Houghton Mifflin Harcourt Publishing Company

Compound Words

doorway	farmworker	heartfelt
housekeeping	paycheck	housework
strawberries	careworn	tarpaper

A. Use the compound words in the box above to help you fill in the missing word part.

1. tar_____

2. _____way

3. _____felt

4. straw_____

5. farm_____

B. Complete each sentence with a word from the box in Part A. Look up any unfamiliar words in the dictionary.

1. The _____ got up early to do his morning chores in the barn.

2. My Grandpa keeps all his tools in a shed whose walls are lined with _____.

3. I love to put slices of juicy _____ on my cereal.

4. Luckily we were able to move the large cabinet through the _____!

5. I wrote a _____ letter to my grandfather to thank him for the old model train set he gave me.

C. Form two new compound words using parts of the compound words in the box below. Write a sentence for each word. Underline the word.

footsteps	waterfall	landscape
daybreak	sunset	gentleman
uphill	outright	seashore

Word 1 _____

_____

_____

Word 2 _____

_____

_____

© Houghton Mifflin Harcourt Publishing Company

Collaborative Discussion Support

Review the selections "Cheated" and "You Work and You Have Nothing" to answer the questions in the chart below.

Questions	My Answers
1. How are Cesar and Dolores alike?	_____ _____ _____ _____ _____ _____ _____
2. What is different about their financial situations?	_____ _____ _____ _____ _____ _____ _____
3. What is different about their reasons for becoming activists when they are grown up?	_____ _____ _____ _____ _____ _____ _____

© Houghton Mifflin Harcourt Publishing Company

Academic Vocabulary

A. Complete each sentence with the correct word from the box.

error	erroneous

1. Not until we got lost did we realize we received _____ directions from the store manager.

error	erroneously

2. While rushing to finish the test on time, Veronika made an _____.

erroneously	erroneous

3. In her report, Jami _____ wrote that Vienna is in Australia.

erroneous	error

4. Be careful using a blog as a resource; it might contain _____ information.

B. Complete each sentence.

1. An example of making an error in judgment might be _____

_____.

2. If I heard erroneous information about someone I would _____

_____.

C. Write about how you have learned from an error you made.

_____

_____

_____

_____

_____

_____

_____

_____

_____

© Houghton Mifflin Harcourt Publishing Company

Critical Vocabulary

A. Read the sentences below. Circle the definition of each underlined word. Remember that you can look up any unfamiliar words in the dictionary.

1. Dolores hoped that attendees would come to <u>occupy</u> every seat, eat every crumb, down every last drop. *Occupy* means

    a. move around.   **b.** sit in.   **c.** put away.

2. Children <u>clung</u> to their parents' hands or dashed ahead to find the best seats. *Clung* means

    a. ran.   **b.** reacted.   **c.** held on.

3. He didn't want to solve everyone's problems; he wanted to help <u>empower</u> the farmworkers to solve their own. *Empower* means

    a. enable.   **b.** encourage.   **c.** involve.

4. The greatest <u>obstacle</u> was the profound lack of resources in the community. *Obstacle* means

    a. benefit.   **b.** difficulty.   **c.** fantasy.

B. Choose a word from the box to complete each sentence.

occupy	empower	clung	uncertainty	union	obstacle

1. Cesar told them that as individuals they couldn't change the situation, but if they formed

    a _____ they would have more power.

2. Having all of us behind you will _____ you to demand your rights.

3. There will always be some _____ in our path, but we have to figure out a way to deal with it.

4. Everyone felt some _____ about the step they were about to take, but they took it anyway.

C. Choose three words from the box in Part B. Use each word in a sentence.

1. _____

   _____

2. _____

   _____

3. _____

   _____

© Houghton Mifflin Harcourt Publishing Company

Synonyms

A. Replace each underlined word with a synonym from the box.

| cognizant | sentiment | component | impact | endeavor | incredulous |

1. Jose believed people should adopt shelter dogs, and luckily his Mom shared this <u>feeling</u>.

_____

2. The class's website on dinosaurs was an <u>effort</u> that took months of work, but the results were

worth it. _____

3. Trees are an important <u>part</u> of the rainforest habitat. _____

4. Janelle was <u>disbelieving</u> when Ms. Richards said a mature tree may have five million active root

tips, but it's a fact. _____

5. Most hikers are <u>aware</u> of the need to drink plenty of water when taking a long hike in hot weather.

_____

B. Complete each sentence with a synonym for each word.

1. A synonym of *incredulous* is _____ .

2. A synonym of *component* is _____ .

3. A synonym of *impact* is _____ .

4. A synonym of *endeavor* is _____ .

5. A synonym of *cognizant* is _____ .

C. Choose two synonym pairs from your answers to Part B. Use each word in a sentence. Underline the synonyms.

1. Synonyms: _____ and _____

_____

_____

_____

2. Synonyms: _____ and _____

_____

_____

_____

© Houghton Mifflin Harcourt Publishing Company

Collaborative Discussion Support

Read the Collaborative Discussion prompt on Student book p. 285 and answer the questions below to complete the chart.

Questions	My Answers
1. Imagine you are at the union-forming meeting in 1962. There are people at the meeting who disagree with Cesar and Dolores. Who might these people be?	
2. What might these opponents say to convince others not to vote for a union?	
3. How might Cesar, Dolores, and their supporters answer the opponents?	
4. In what way would Cesar and Dolores need to speak in order to persuade listeners that their opponents are wrong and they are right?	

USE WITH STUDENT BOOK pp. 278–283

© Houghton Mifflin Harcourt Publishing Company

Affixes

beautiful	successful	disagreement	inadvisibility	happiness	uncertain

A. Choose a word from the box to answer each question.

1. Which word describes a difference of opinion? _____

2. Which word describes the riskiness of an action that is not recommended? _____

3. Which word describes the state of people filled with joy? _____

4. Which word describes a person who attains a goal? _____

5. Which word would you use to describe an event whose outcome is not sure? _____

6. Which word describes a sight or state that is very pleasing? _____

B. Complete each sentence with a word from the box.

1. By the eighth inning, the score was tied, so the outcome of the game was still _____.

2. Melanie gasped with delight seeing the _____ colors of the autumn trees.

3. Considering that the pond might not be fully frozen, Josh had to agree with his sister on the _____ of skating.

4. Our class was the most _____ at the charity event, raising over $200 for the local animal shelter.

5. My sister and I had a _____ about which dog to adopt, since she wanted the poodle and I liked the beagle.

C. Choose three words from the box at the top of the page. Use each word in a sentence.

1. _____
   _____

2. _____
   _____

3. _____
   _____

© Houghton Mifflin Harcourt Publishing Company

Misuse of Adjectives and Adverbs

A. **Decide which word to use. Circle the correct word.**

1. Tina has [real, really] long hair: it reaches to her waist.

2. Chris has [never, neverly] seen this band perform live.

3. I did [good, well] on the test.

4. This desk has [fewer, less] space than the one I used to have.

B. **Fill in the blank with an adjective or adverb that makes sense.**

1. Is that a _____ shark tooth?

2. Cath _____ eats meat.

3. This game has much _____ combat than most of the games I play.

4. I feel _____ about making you wait.

5. Lizzy plays the piano _____ because of her years of practice.

C. **Choose one topic and write four sentences about it. Use at least four of the adjectives or adverbs.**

Possible topics:

how you'd like to celebrate your birthday	something you are an optimist about	reasons you would want to be friends with someone

1. _____

_____

2. _____

_____

3. _____

_____

4. _____

_____

© Houghton Mifflin Harcourt Publishing Company

Speak Out!

To evaluate your oral argument, use the Oral Argument Rubric available from your online Student Resources or from your teacher.

A. Plan Your Oral Argument

1. Answer the following questions (these are questions for your whole group):

   a. Will you have each group member present one piece of information? Yes No (Circle one.)

   If so, what main idea(s) will each person talk about?_____

   _____

   _____

   _____

   b. Which group member will summarize your argument?_____

   _____

   c. Which group member will answer listeners' questions?_____

   _____

2. In your group, discuss the following topics. One group member can take notes.

   a. What are some of the hardships farmworkers face? _____

   _____

   _____

   _____

   b. How could a union help solve farmworkers' problems?

   _____

   _____

   _____

   _____

B. Write Your Oral Argument

Use your notes from Part A, Item 2 to write your argument on another sheet of paper. If you like, you can copy your final draft onto index cards to make your argument easier to present. Remember to include:

- an opening statement that says your group is FOR a strong union for farmworkers
- reasons why you support forming a union, and facts to support your reasons
- a closing statement that sums up your oral argument

© Houghton Mifflin Harcourt Publishing Company

Deconstruct a Sentence

Reread the sentence below from page 280 of "Viva La Causa." Then answer the questions to help you deconstruct the sentence (take it apart) and put it back together.

"He didn't want to solve everyone's problems; he wanted to empower the farmworkers to solve their own, and that empowerment was impossible without the formation of a union."

Questions	My Answers
1. Who is "he" in this sentence?	
2. What did he want?	
3. What did he *not* want?	
4. What does it mean to *empower* someone to do something?	
5. What did he believe he and others had to do in order to "empower the farmworkers to solve their own [problems]"?	
6. Restate the whole sentence in your own words. (You can write more than one sentence.)	

© Houghton Mifflin Harcourt Publishing Company

Academic Vocabulary

A. Decide if each statement indicates an adequate or inadequate amount of something for the situation. Complete the chart by writing *adequate* or *inadequate*.

Situation	Adequate/Inadequate
The only copy of a book you want is checked out from the library.	
Your report lacks sources to back up the facts.	
He likes being well-prepared for an exam.	
He had a small heater for a big room.	
There's plenty of medicine to cure an infection.	

B. Complete the answers with information from the text. Use either *adequate* or *inadequate* in your response.

> One city is trying a new method of mosquito control because past efforts were inadequate in preventing diseases spread by mosquitoes. Ponds and lakes will be filled with new fish that eat mosquito larvae to see if this will adequately control the mosquito population. Some scientists worry that the effect the new fish will have on the ecosystem has been inadequately studied. City officials said they are anxious to test the adequacy of this new method in the battle against mosquito-borne diseases.

1. Why is the city trying a new method of mosquito control?

It is trying a new method because past efforts _____

_____.

2. What do they hope the new fish will do?

They hope the new fish will _____.

3. Why are some scientists worried about the effect of the new fish?

Scientists worry that the effect the new fish will have _____

_____.

4. What are city officials anxious to test?

They are anxious to test _____

_____.

C. Complete the sentences.

1. The adequate supply of party refreshments will ensure that the guests _____.

2. Inadequate sleep can be a problem for students because _____.

© Houghton Mifflin Harcourt Publishing Company

Critical Vocabulary

A. Read the sentences below. Circle the definition of each underlined word. Remember that you can look up any unfamiliar words in the dictionary.

1. The green knight held up his <u>severed</u> head like a lantern, got on his horse, and rode away. *Severed* means

    a. detached.   **b.** attached.   **c.** dying.

2. Sir Gawain was confused; <u>nevertheless</u>, he agreed. *Nevertheless* means

    a. already.   **b.** so.   **c.** even so.

3. <u>Gradually</u> the form of a man took shape in the distance. *Gradually* means

    a. suddenly.   **b.** little by little.   **c.** barely.

4. It was love that made you <u>conceal</u> the belt from me, so that you might live! *Conceal* means

    a. reveal.   **b.** hide.   **c.** steal.

B. Choose a word from the box to complete each sentence.

axe	gradually	severed	fulfill	nevertheless	conceal

1. Craig made a promise to his father, and he plans to _____ it.

2. Dorothy is a talented violinist; _____ she has to practice.

3. The farmer used an _____ to chop down the tree in the middle of his field.

4. The knight tried to _____ his true identity by wearing a mask.

C. Choose three words from the box in Part B. Use each word in a sentence. Write the sentence.

1. _____

   _____

2. _____

   _____

3. _____

   _____

© Houghton Mifflin Harcourt Publishing Company

Visual Clues

weary	chamber	pheasant	blustery	craggy	brambles

A. Choose the best word from the box to complete each sentence.

1. The travelers found that March winds made for _____ weather.

   a. craggy   **b.** blustery

2. In the woods, the hikers ran into a patch of _____ and Michael's bare legs got scratched by the branches.

   a. pheasant   **b.** brambles

3. After discussing where to spend the night, the _____ travelers stopped at the nearest inn.

   a. weary   **b.** blustery

4. In the historic house, we loved the beautiful furnishings and colors of the lady's _____ .

   a. chamber   **b.** pheasant

5. The _____ peaks of the mountains had been worn down to jagged rocks by thousands of years of erosion.

   a. craggy   **b.** weary

B. Write the word from the box at the top of the page that most closely fits each of the following descriptions of an illustration.

1. a furnished bedroom in old house _____

2. a large bird that looks a little like a chicken _____

3. a mountain that is rough and rocky _____

4. low shrubs with thorny branches _____

5. tree branches blowing in gusts of wind _____

C. Choose three words from the box. Use each word in a sentence that is <u>not</u> about the tale of Sir Gawain and the Green Knight.

1. _____

   _____

2. _____

   _____

3. _____

   _____

© Houghton Mifflin Harcourt Publishing Company

Collaborative Discussion Support

Complete the following chart. Some boxes have been filled in for you.

page/ frame	Information from the Text About Sir Gawain's Quest	What This Text Tells You About Gawain's Quest and Quests in General
p. 287 frame 3	"I challenge you, King Arthur. Take this axe and strike me with it as hard as you can! If I survive, you'll allow me to do the same to you in a year's time."	When Gawain beheads the Green Knight, he makes a bargain with the giant — the same bargain the Green Knight challenged King Arthur to make with him.
p. 289 frame 3	_____ _____ _____ _____	By the end of the story, this agreement with his host turns out to be part of Sir Gawain's quest. The host is setting up a test for his visitor, but Sir Gawain doesn't know that he is about to be tested.
p. 289 frame 5	"I love you, Sir Gawain.... Please take me away with you!"	_____ _____ _____
p. 290 frame 5	_____ _____ _____	_____ _____ _____
p. 291 frame 5	_____ _____ _____	_____ _____ _____
p. 292 frame 2	_____ _____ _____ _____	_____ _____ _____ _____
p. 293 frame 1	_____ _____ _____	_____ _____ _____

© Houghton Mifflin Harcourt Publishing Company

Word Families

| respond | respondent | irresponsive | responsibility |

A. Choose a word from the box to answer each question.

1. Which word means "someone who answers"? _____

2. Which word means "a duty"? _____

3. Which word means "to answer"? _____

4. Which word means "not responding"? _____

B. Complete each sentence with the correct word from the box at the top of the page.

1. It's Alex's _____ to help clean up the dishes after dinner.

2. The _____ answered all of the judge's questions.

3. I think the reason Mr. Izod was _____ to your question is because he did not hear you.

4. Please raise your hand in class to _____ to the teacher's question.

C. Choose two words from the box and write a sentence for each word.

1. _____

_____

_____

2. _____

_____

_____

© Houghton Mifflin Harcourt Publishing Company

Identify Prepositions in Difficult Sentences

A. Identify the subject of the sentence, removing prepositional phrases to help you find it. Circle the correct answer.

1. The book with the blue cover has been read by many people all over the world.

   a. blue   **b.** book   **c.** people   **d.** world

2. Racing toward the finish line, Sarah realized she could win by maintaining focus on her goal.

   a. Sarah   **b.** focus   **c.** line   **d.** goal

3. Without a map, we'll have to use our phones to find our way around this neighborhood.

   a. map   **b.** neighborhood   **c.** phones   **d.** we

4. At parties, Sandy likes to talk to everyone in the room.

   a. room   **b.** parties   **c.** Sandy   **d.** everyone

B. Cross out all the prepositional phrases in the sentence.

1. Despite all the warnings, the group ventured into the deep forest.

2. You can find lots of extra blankets for guests in the chest behind the couch.

3. Melissa, unlike her sisters, goes to school across town.

4. The clues in the first few chapters of the mystery novel flew right over my head.

5. Before school, Jaya gets dressed with care and eats a breakfast of hot cereal.

C. Choose one topic and write four sentences about it. Use at least one prepositional phrase per sentence.

Possible topics:

what you think is most important in a friend	your favorite historical figure	what kind of unusual animal you'd like to have as a pet

1. _____

   _____

2. _____

   _____

3. _____

   _____

4. _____

   _____

© Houghton Mifflin Harcourt Publishing Company

Analyze the Text

Answer each question. Write evidence from the selection that supports each of your answers. Read the Analyzing the Text Prompt on p. 294 of the Student Book to complete the chart.

Question 1	My Answer	Evidence from page 287, frame 4
Interpret What does he mean when Sir Gawain tells himself he has done the right thing to take the Green Knight's challenge, no matter his fate?		

Question 2	My Answer	Evidence from page 293, frame 2
Identify What do you learn about the identity of the Green Knight?		

Question 3	My Answer	Evidence from page 293, frames 3 and 4
Compare How does the way Sir Gawain feels about his scar differ from the way the Knight feels about it?		

© Houghton Mifflin Harcourt Publishing Company

Base Words

youngest	traveler	protest	visitor	severed	roamed

A. Choose a word from the box to answer each question.

1. Which word means "a person who goes takes a journey"? _____

2. Which word means "least old"? _____

3. Which word means "cut off"? _____

4. Which word means "to express strong objections to something"? _____

5. Which word means "moved around without purpose"? _____

B. Complete the sentences with the correct word from the box.

youngest	traveler	protest	visitor	severed	roamed

1. I wrote a letter to the newspaper to _____ the planned closing of our neighborhood park.

2. We had a _____ from next door yesterday, when a neighbor's cat leaped into our kitchen window.

3. The hurricane ripped through the garden, and the heads of many flowers were _____ from their stems.

4. I always get hand-me-downs to wear from my older sisters, since I'm the _____ in the family.

5. My uncle Gene was a great _____ who toured countries as far apart as Japan, Norway, and South Africa.

C. Write three sentences. In each sentence use one word from the box.

1. _____

_____

2. _____

_____

3. _____

_____

© Houghton Mifflin Harcourt Publishing Company

Oral Argument Topics

A. Here are the selections from this unit. Pick three and write a claim related to each of your choices.

"DogGone"

"Claudette Colvin" from *Freedom Walkers: The Story of the Montgomery Bus Boycott*

"A Change of Plans"

"You Work and You Have Nothing" from *La Causa*

"Viva la Causa" from *La Causa*

"Sir Gawain and the Green Knight"

1. _____
   _____

2. _____
   _____

3. _____
   _____

B. Write three possible topics for your oral argument.

Idea 1 _____
_____
_____

Idea 2 _____
_____
_____

Idea 3 _____
_____
_____

© Houghton Mifflin Harcourt Publishing Company

Plan Your Oral Argument

Make a Claim and Present Reasons

Write your claim as a statement. Think of a clear and interesting way to state it.

_____

What facts and opinions from the selections will support your claim?

_____

_____

_____

What facts and opinions from other sources could you use?

_____

_____

_____

Identify Possible Counterarguments

What might someone say to oppose your claim?

_____

_____

_____

What facts and opinions from the selections or other sources could you use to oppose the counterarguments?

_____

_____

_____

Prepare for Speaking Aloud

What must you focus on in order to make a convincing presentation? (Examples: making eye contact with the audience, speaking with expression, using gestures.)

_____

_____

_____

Think About Style

Are there any words related to your claim that you may need to explain?

_____

_____

© Houghton Mifflin Harcourt Publishing Company

Academic Vocabulary

A. Complete each sentence with the correct word from the box.

| interact | interaction | interactive |

1. Quiet children tend not to _____ much with their peers.

2. An _____ map on the computer can convey types of information better than a paper map.

3. Miles was happy to observe the friendly _____ among the guests at his party.

4. Some people prefer to _____ over the Internet rather than in person.

B. Complete each sentence.

1. My favorite kind of social interaction is _____ because _____
_____
_____.

2. One way human interaction can be more effective than email interaction is _____
_____
_____.

C. Using the words from the box, write about an interaction you have had with a member of another species.

_____
_____
_____

© Houghton Mifflin Harcourt Publishing Company

Finalize Your Plan

SPEAKING TOOLBOX

Elements of an Oral Argument

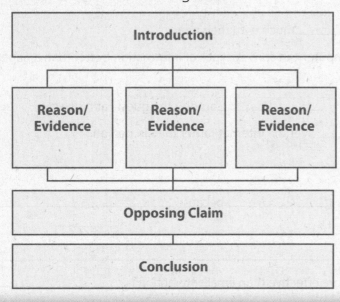

Introduction	Present your claim as a statement. Include an interesting fact, question, or quotation to get your listeners' attention.
Reason/ Evidence **Reason/ Evidence** **Reason/ Evidence**	Present each reason in a logical order. Make sure the reasons are logical and relevant. They could be facts or opinions, from the selections or from other credible sources.
Opposing Claim	Identify a possible opposite point of view. Use facts and evidence to dispute it.
Conclusion	The conclusion should restate your claim and sum up your reasons supporting it.

A. Review the elements of an oral argument above. Then describe the elements that you will include in your presentation.

Introduction _____

_____

Reasons/Evidence _____

_____

Opposing Claim _____

_____

Conclusion _____

_____

B. Write a brief summary of your argument.

_____

_____

_____

_____

© Houghton Mifflin Harcourt Publishing Company

Vocabulary Review

Here are some of the words you learned in this unit. Choose words from this list and sort them into the categories below. There are many possible correct answers! Also, many of the words fit into more than one category.

barriers	empower	integrated	shelter
battery	entitled	lodging	toiling
berating	equestrian	mimic	toll
brambles	erroneous	patient	traveler
broom	farmworkers	paycheck	unacceptable
canine	gradually	pheasant	union
careworn	heartache	plowed	unjust
conceal	housework	protest	visitor
despite	inadequate	roamed	wage
doorway	inadvisability	segregation	wear

Multiple-Meaning Words

1. Word: _____

   Definition 1: _____

   Definition 2: _____

2. Word: _____

   Definition 1: _____

   Definition 2: _____

Words with Prefixes

1. _____

2. _____

3. _____

4. _____

5. _____

Compound Words

1. _____

2. _____

3. _____

4. _____

5. _____

Nouns

1. _____

2. _____

3. _____

4. _____

5. _____

© Houghton Mifflin Harcourt Publishing Company

Easily Confused Words

whose	who's	loose	lose	foreward	forward

A. Circle the correct word in each sentence. Use the context clues to help you decide.

1. [Whose, Who's] ringing the doorbell?

2. I have a [loose, lose] thread on my jacket.

3. Did you already [loose, lose] your winter gloves?

4. This author writes in the [forward, foreword] that her book is intended for all kinds of readers.

B. Fill in the blanks with the correct word from the box that fits the context of the sentence.

1. Even if you suffer setbacks, you have to keep moving _____.

2. _____ car is parked in front of the driveway?

3. I think we can _____ the people following us if we turn here.

4. The sweater is a little _____ on her, but I think it fits.

5. I don't know _____ sending me these messages, but I want them to stop.

C. Write four sentences that each use a word from the box above. Your sentences should demonstrate your understanding of the meaning of each word.

1. _____
_____
_____

2. _____
_____
_____

3. _____
_____
_____

4. _____
_____
_____

© Houghton Mifflin Harcourt Publishing Company